simple gifts
to stitch

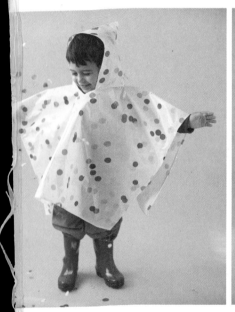

simple gifts to stitch

30 Elegant and Easy Projects

Jocelyn Worrall

Photography by Alexandra Grablewski

POTTER
CRAFT

new york

Copyright © 2007 by Jocelyn Worrall
Published in the United States by Potter Craft, an imprint of
the Crown Publishing Group, a division of Random House, Inc., New York.
www.crownpublishing.com
www.pottercraft.com
POTTER CRAFT is a trademark, and POTTER CRAFT and colophon
are registered trademarks of Random House, Inc.
Library of Congress Cataloging-in-Publication Data

Worrall, Jocelyn.
Simple gifts to stitch : 30 elegant and easy projects / Jocelyn Worrall ;
photography by Alexandra Grablewski. — 1st ed.
p. cm.
Includes index.
ISBN: 978-0-307-34756-5
1. Sewing. 2. Needlework—Patterns. 3. Gifts. I. Title.
TT715.W65 2007
746—dc22
2006028124

ISBN 978-0-307-34756-5
Printed in China
Design by Lauren Monchik
Photographs by Alexandra Grablewski
1 3 5 7 9 10 8 6 4 2
First Edition

THIS BOOK IS DEDICATED TO

Splitchani

Silas Ulysses

Margaret Dominica Olsen

contents

introduction

Many years ago, I needed a gift for my friend's wedding. I was broke, but I had a huge pile of fabric accumulating in my apartment from my job as a textile designer. So I made a quilt. I used an army blanket for batting and otherwise improvised my way to my first successful, simple, stitched gift. I discovered that handmade gifts are less expensive, more appreciated, and, best of all, can be tailored to the individual.

Like many people, I am a great procrastinator when it comes to working on my own projects. But when I want to make something for someone else, I somehow spring into action. It's just more enjoyable. It's like cooking—who likes to cook for themselves? So these days, when I find myself needing a gift, I begin by sifting through my collection of fabrics and swatches and writing down my ideas in a sketchbook.

I admit to being obsessed with textiles, and many of my ideas begin with the intrinsic beauty of a particular fabric. Linen is one of my favorites. Not only do I love its historical significance—it's one of the oldest textiles known—but I also appreciate how beautifully it ages. The next time you are at a flea market, look for an antique linen pillowcase and notice its amazing buttery texture. As much as I love fabrics made with natural fibers, I also appreciate modern synthetic fabrics, especially those that are obviously synthetic, like oilcloth and vinyl. For this book, I picked materials I love and tried to bring out their unique qualities. I asked myself questions like: How can I make use of this water-resistant, non-fraying material that comes in many colors? Or how can yards of that standard craft trimming, rickrack, be transformed into an elegant object? I tried to come up with designs that I felt were slightly unusual but practical. I brainstormed techniques. Sculpture and origami inspired some of the projects, as I like to look at fabric as a material similar to paper or a sheet of metal. I thought about the many ingenious needlecraft traditions that preceded the invention of the sewing machine, like cross-stitch and pulled-and-drawn thread.

The sewing machine is an amazing tool with great versatility. What I love is that you can use the sewing machine in a simple, spontaneous way or in a very precise and planned way. In both cases, you can make something

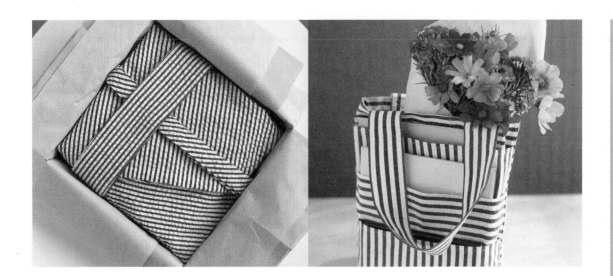

incredible, whether it's made from fabric scraps, lengths of ribbon, expensive wool, or even paper. Sewing is like carpentry: You create something amazing by joining materials together. Even some of the terms are the same like mitered corners and grain. Sewing, though, because it's on a smaller, less expensive, and less dangerous scale, allows for much more experimentation. While every project in this book is like a recipe, with detailed instructions and a list of the items and tools needed to make it, I also hope that the projects inspire you to add your own ideas.

Since I am self-taught and would describe my sewing skills as "intuitional," the projects are all based on very simple concepts. Some may require more time than others, but are less complex. Others may call for more concentration during preparation, but can then be sewn together in minutes. Many of the designs may be easily elaborated on, and most of the projects can be done in an afternoon or less. If you plan on making something again, remember that it's always quicker the second time around. It just gets easier, and maybe you'll discover a shortcut, or change something to make it even better.

I am always enticing my friends with wine and food to get them to come over and sew with me. I love working in a social setting, with music blaring and my son running around, creating chaos. However it works for you, the most important thing is to start sewing immediately because you are just so excited. It's about making something completely satisfying with a simple plan and a bit of verve.

THINGS TO KNOW
BEFORE YOU SEW

Before you begin, read through the suggestions below to help make your sewing experience go smoothly.

1. Spend some time in fabric stores looking around and collecting swatches that strike you, even if you have no particular project in mind. Keep a box of fabric swatches for inspiration, and turn to it when you're planning a project. In a perfect world, all the swatches would be marked with the price, the width, and the store they came from. If that's asking too much, just storing them all in one place is a big step in the right direction.

2. Wash the fabric before you embark on your sewing project. Many fabrics are treated with a chemical "sizing" (a water-soluble finishing agent used in the manufacturing process) that you want to remove, and many fabrics shrink when washed. The fabric will just end up shrinking after you've spent all that time sewing it perfectly. Trim the raw edges with pinking shears before washing, to prevent the threads from becoming a tangled mess in the dryer.

3. Iron the fabric before cutting. This will help you to measure and cut with accuracy. Use a press cloth and adjust the iron temperature as needed. Fabrics like linen and cotton require steam or a misting of water with a spray bottle to remove the creases.

4. Use a press cloth when pressing with an iron. A small square of muslin or another lightweight cotton makes an ideal press cloth. It should be thin enough to allow the steam and heat to move through it to press your fabric, yet provide enough of a barrier to prevent the fabric from getting scorched or stained by a dirty iron.

5. Use a clean iron when pressing, even if you are using a press cloth. Irons pick up dirt and residue from fabrics, and you might occasionally melt something under your iron! Clean the iron with iron cleaner and a cloth, available at housewares stores.

6. Measure twice, cut once is a golden rule in carpentry as well as sewing. This rule cannot be emphasized enough. Once you measure and mark the fabric, do it again! It is also a good idea to keep a sewing notebook to jot down the measurements and cut-sizes of projects for future reference. You may want to make them again.

7. Use a rotary cutter instead of scissors. Now that I have discovered the rotary cutter, I almost never use scissors. A rotary cutter is used in conjunction with a cutting mat and a ruler, and will give you the straightest, most precise cuts. It is especially useful when cutting a fine, slippery fabric, and when you need to make long, straight cuts in fabric.

8. Use a clear quilter's (acrylic) ruler and a cutting mat in conjunction with a rotary cutter. It is ideal to have a few different ruler sizes, but 6" × 24" (15 × 61cm) is a good basic size. Using a clear ruler allows you to line up the ruler marks with the lines on the cutting mat, making it very easy to measure and cut right angles. The clear ruler and cutting mat also lets you trim excess fabric on a seam allowance in seconds. Cutting mats come in a variety of sizes; a large one is ideal. A 36" × 24" mat will measure a yard length and the diagonal lines enable you to cut fabric at a perfect 45-degree angle.

9. Always pin in the same direction, the one that allows you to pull the pins out from the

fabric just before stitching over them. I can honestly say that I often stitch over the pins, but this is not recommended. You will hit a pin every once in a while, and when this happens, the needle may become bent (if it doesn't break entirely) and result in irregular stitches, so beware. As a rule, I always pin perpendicular to the stitch line, with the pins pointing in toward the center of the fabric. On occasion, it will make more sense to pin along the stitch line; in those cases it will be obvious. There are several types of straight pins out there: Quilting pins are extra long and are great for pinning thick fabrics, and the classic ball-head pins are great for all other fabrics.

10. Test the stitching on a small piece of the fabric before you start to sew your project. You may need to adjust the tension on your sewing machine, the stitch length or width, or the size of the needle.

11. Match the spool thread and the bobbin thread. The two should be from the same spool, or the same brand and type of thread. Sometimes, you may want to use green for the top stitch, and blue for the bottom stitch (for aesthetic reasons).

12. Wind the bobbins ahead of time if you are working on a project requiring a lot of sewing. That way you don't have to stop and wind when the bobbin runs out. Some machines allow simultaneous winding of the bobbin as you are sewing. This sounds dreamy, but I could never seem to make use of this feature.

13. Keep a dish for pins next to your machine. As you are sewing and removing the pins, place them in a dish or a pincushion. I do this and somehow I still end up with pins all over the house, though it helps!

14. Press the finished project when you're done, on appropriate fabrics of course. Invest in a great steam iron and keep it clean. A nice pressing makes a big difference and will really make the project shine.

FOUR SIMPLE TECHNIQUES

HOW TO MAKE A BUTTONHOLE

Test the buttonhole on a fabric scrap before stitching one on the actual project. Using fabric chalk or a fabric marker, mark the fabric with a single line the length of the buttonhole, which should match the diameter of the button plus a little extra. Set the sewing machine to zigzag stitch. To determine the appropriate stitch width and length, test the stitch on a fabric scrap. Adjust the tension if needed. Sew along either side of the buttonhole mark, leaving a bit less than $\frac{1}{16}$" (1.6 mm) in between the two lines. Set the stitch width to a slightly wider stitch to sew a few wide stitches at either end of the buttonhole. Cut the buttonhole center, using small, sharp scissors. If you inadvertently cut the threads, stitch over them again.

HOW TO SEW ON A BUTTON

Begin by sewing with the knot on the right side of the fabric; it will be hidden under the button. Leave a tiny amount of thread in between the button and the fabric in order to create some space for the fabric being fastened to the button. Pass the thread through the holes in the button several times and then wind the thread around itself between the button and the fabric to form a shank. When using thinner fabrics, make a shorter shank; for thicker fabrics, make a longer shank. Knot the thread by locking it with several more stitches, ending on the right side of the fabric, just under the button.

HOW TO SEW A DOUBLE HEM

Many projects in this book require sewing a $\frac{1}{4}$" (6mm) double hem, which is essentially using a $\frac{1}{2}$" (13mm) seam allowance. The more often you do this, the easier it becomes to eyeball $\frac{1}{4}$" (6mm). If you are not comfortable eyeballing the measurement, mark the fabric edges with fabric chalk or a fabric marker using a long, clear ruler in two measures: $\frac{1}{4}$" (6mm) and $\frac{1}{2}$" (13mm) from the edge. If hemming a hardcore synthetic material like vinyl, it's probably best not to press the hem with an iron—either pin the hem into place or fold it over by hand while sewing. Otherwise, with most natural fiber fabrics, you can first press the fabric with your finger to create a faint crease. This is something you do as you go along the hem, just before you iron a section. After pressing the $\frac{1}{4}$" (6mm) hem, fold the fabric over $\frac{1}{4}$" (6mm) (the fold should be along the $\frac{1}{2}$" [13mm] marked line) and press again. You have just used $\frac{1}{2}$" (13mm) of seam allowance, or created a $\frac{1}{4}$" (6mm) double hem. You may or may not need to pin the hem before sewing, depending on the fabric. It is generally a good idea to pin, even if the fabric requires just a few, as fabric tends to migrate, or shift, during the sewing. You decide if you want to wing it or play it safe. Sew the hem as close as possible to the inner folded edge, without straying into the non-hem area.

HOW TO SEW ENCASEMENTS (WHEN SEWING TWO FABRICS TOGETHER TO TURN RIGHT-SIDE OUT)

Anytime you are sewing a pillow or anything that requires sewing two fabrics together, right sides together, think about the placement for the opening that you will need to leave in order to turn the piece right-side out. There is always an ideal place. For instance, when sewing projects with corners, like pillows, always sew the corners and place the opening somewhere along one side, at least a few inches from a corner. This way all the corners will look the same.

Trim away any extra fabric at the corners and on the seam allowance before turning right-side out. Be careful not to cut too close to the seam. Don't trim fragile fabrics that fray and unravel easily, or any project that will experience excessive wear and laundering. If possible, press the seam allowance around the opening before hand-sewing it closed. That way the fabric seams will match cleanly and the hand-sewn closure will be imperceptible.

Use a slipstitch to close the opening. Place the two fabric seams together and pin the opening closed. Draw the thread up from the wrong side and begin stitching by piercing through both fabrics on the seam and sewing a tiny stitch on the fold, picking up only two or three threads of each fabric. Space the stitches $1/8''$ (3mm) apart for finer fabrics or $1/4''$ (6mm) apart for heavier fabrics. When you're done, press the area of the hand-sewn opening lightly.

GLOSSARY

TECHNIQUES AND TERMS

bias: A true bias runs at a 45-degree angle to the straight grain of the fabric. Fabric cut on the bias drapes more fluidly and has more stretch. Raw edges will fray much less when cut on the bias.

binding: A length of fabric, either in a single or double layer, used to finish raw edges. Binding is usually cut on the bias so that it is slightly stretchy.

cross-stitch: A decorative hand-sewing technique consisting of two stitches that cross to form an X.

dart: A stitched triangular fold in the material, used to give shape and form to the fabric. Often used in garments to fit curves of the body.

ease: An even distribution of fullness when a piece of fabric is joined to a slightly smaller piece.

fringe: A decorative edge formed by pulling the warp or weft threads away from the fabric.

grain: The direction of the warp threads. Usually refers to the lengthwise direction of the fabric, how it comes off the loom. Cross-grain is the opposite, the direction of the weft threads.

hem: A finished edge made by folding back the raw edge of the fabric and stitching it by machine or by hand.

machine quilting: Using the sewing machine to quilt by topstitching over the fabric and batting.

mitered corner: A corner created by joining the fabric with a seam at a 45-degree angle.

nap: A very subtle, fuzzy surface on a fabric, created by raised fibers.

pintucks: Tiny pleats stitched close to a folded edge, usually used for decorative purposes.

placket: A finished opening, usually closed with buttons, snaps, or zippers.

pleats: Folds in a fabric made by doubling the material on itself, then pressing or stitching into place.

pulled and drawn threads: A centuries-old embroidery technique for which select threads are pulled and drawn out from the fabric. These areas are then embroidered over, creating a decorative lacy effect.

seam allowance: The fabric that extends beyond the stitching line, often $1/4''$ (6mm) or more if the fabric is coarsely woven. An ample seam allowance is essential for preventing the stitches from falling out. Fragile fabric should have the seam allowance zigzag-stitched to prevent it from fraying.

selvedge: The tightly woven border on the lengthwise edges of the fabric.

shank: The "stem" between the button and the fabric to which it is sewn. May be a part of the button or may be created by wrapping the thread around itself, like a cord, when sewing the button on.

shirring: Parallel rows of machine- or hand-stitching gathered to create a textural effect.

slash: Straight lines cut into fabric, usually into the seam allowance (perpendicular to the stitch line), for easing curves or angles.

slipstitch: Tiny, almost invisible hand-stitches sewn through and under a fabric fold.

tack: A small stitch or stitches, done by machine or hand, used to secure fabrics together at a particular point.

topstitching: A line of stitching on the right side of the fabric, often decorative or sewn along a finished seam or edge.

trapunto: A centuries-old Italian quilting technique in which only the designs on the fabric are padded, producing a raised, decorative surface.

wale: The rib or raised cord that runs lengthwise on the grain of a corduroy fabric. Used in reference to the width of the rib (i.e., wide wale or narrow wale).

warp: The threads stretched under tension on a loom. Warp threads run the length of a fabric.

weft: The threads woven into the warp, shot across a loom in shuttles. Weft threads run across the width of a fabric.

whipstitch: Hand-sewn stitch used for finishing or joining raw edges or for attaching trimmings. Whipstitches are worked right to left, taking diagonal stitches over the edge(s).

TOOLS, NOTIONS, AND MATERIALS

batting: The layer of stuffing between the top and bottom layers of a quilt, available in various lofts, in cotton, polyester, and wool.

bone folder: A bookbinding tool that resembles a letter opener, made of bone. An excellent tool for pushing out corners in sewn casements (like a pillow), though a chopstick or the blunt end of a pencil will do the job, too. Can be found at art supply stores and bookbinding supply stores.

cutting mat (self-healing mat): A plastic/rubber work mat printed with a grid of measurements, available in several sizes. Used in conjunction with a rotary cutter and a quilter's ruler for cutting fabric.

elastic: A flexible band of woven rubber threads available in various widths, weights, textures, and colors.

embroidery floss: Thick, mercerized cotton thread composed of six strands of thread, available in a wide range of colors.

embroidery hoop: A pair of wooden or plastic rings, one fitting inside the other, available in various sizes. Fabric is stretched taut between the two rings, allowing for precise and controlled hand-stitching.

fabric marker: A special pen with ink that disappears after a few hours; used for making temporary marks on fabric. Always test on fabric before using.

fiber filling: Lightweight synthetic fiber used as stuffing.

fray check: A liquid seam sealant used on ribbon ends to prevent fraying.

handkerchief linen: A thin, lightweight linen, usually of very high quality.

hook-and-loop tape (Velcro): A fastening material consisting of two layers—a hook side, which is a piece of fabric covered with tiny plastic hooks, and a loop side, which is covered in equally tiny soft loops. Available in a variety of colors and widths.

interfacing: A stiff woven or non-woven material used to stabilize or reinforce fabrics. Usually available in black, white, or gray. Fusible interfacing has an adhesive coating on one side that adheres to fabric when ironed.

iron-on vinyl: Clear plastic vinyl that adheres permanently to fabric when the heat of an iron is applied.

pinking shears: Scissors with zigzag blades, often used to finish fabric edges to help prevent or delay threads from fraying.

press cloth: A square of light cloth placed in between a hot iron and the fabric being pressed, to protect the fabric from scorching. A piece of lightweight muslin makes an excellent press cloth.

quilter's ruler (acrylic ruler): A clear plastic ruler available in various lengths and widths, the quilter's ruler is an excellent tool for cutting precise lines and right angles. It is used in conjunction with a rotary cutter and a cutting mat.

quilting pins: Extra-long straight pins used for quilting or pinning thick fabrics.

rotary cutter: A tool with a circular cutting blade used with a cutting mat and a ruler to make very precise cuts. This tool is invaluable for cutting slippery fabrics like silk or nylon.

seam ripper: A small, sharp metal tool used for undoing stitches.

sewing needles: Hand-sewing needles vary in the size of the eye, the length, and the thickness of their points. They are generally sold in a packet of various lengths and sizes. Always have a range of sizes on hand. Machine-sewing needles vary in size as well, and fall into two general categories. The ballpoint needle, usually marked "B" or "BP" on the package, is for sewing knits, and the regular needle is for sewing all other fabrics. Machine needles vary in size from 9, for fine, thin fabrics, to 18, for heavier, thick fabrics.

tailor's chalk: Water-soluble chalk used to mark fabric. Though it is designed to brush off, always test it on fabric before using.

FABRICS

broadcloth: A plain, finely woven fabric usually made from cotton, a polyester/cotton blend, silk, or wool. Cotton broadcloth resembles sheeting fabric and is usually available in a variety of colors. The finest qualities are made with combed Pima or Egyptian cotton.

canvas: Strong, stiff woven fabric usually made of cotton or nylon. Canvas is good for making items that will withstand heavy-duty use.

cashmere: An extremely soft, expensive woven or knit fabric made from the downy fleece of Asian goats.

chambray: A seemingly solid-color woven fabric composed of two different-colored yarns. The warp is one solid color and the weft is another solid color. Chambray can often have an iridescent effect, depending on the color combination.

corduroy: Durable, soft woven fabric with lengthwise cords of pile in various widths, usually made of cotton fibers.

cotton: Absorbent, soft woven or knit fabric made with fibers from the cotton plant.

dotted swiss: Finely woven, sheer cotton fabric, originally from Switzerland, flecked with tiny plush dots.

faux fur: Plush fabric made of artificial fibers designed to look like real animal fur; also known as synthetic fur.

felt: Dense fabric composed of wool or synthetic fiber staples made by compressing the fiber with heat and moisture.

flannel: A woven material, usually cotton, with a soft, napped surface.

fleece: A thick, soft, felted synthetic fabric. Fleece is often used for winter wear due to its wool-like feel and insulating qualities.

gingham: A woven fabric with two vertical and horizontal colored yarns forming a check effect. The most common check size is about $1/4''$ (6mm), but it is available in a variety of sizes.

grosgrain (ribbon): A ribbed, tightly woven fabric of silk or rayon particular to ribbon. Often used for trimming clothing and hats.

jersey: A soft, thin knit fabric made from cotton, rayon, silk, linen, wool, or synthetic fibers.

lambswool: A soft, fine woven or knit fabric made from the fleece of young sheep. Lambswool is a less expensive alternative to cashmere.

linen: Woven or knit fabric made from the fibers of the flax plant. Linen is available in a variety of weights, textures, and grades. It is strong and durable, and softens with age.

moiré: A fabric finished with a process that gives it a wavy, watermarked appearance. Moiré is often seen on grosgrain ribbon.

muslin: An inexpensive, widely available, plain-weave cotton fabric, often used to mock up designs before making them from the actual fabric.

oilcloth: A manmade, mesh-backed vinyl material that is shiny in appearance and waterproof.

rayon: A manmade fiber derived from natural plant material (cellulose), primarily from trees. Rayon takes dye very well and also drapes well.

rickrack: A saw-toothed-edge trimming available in a variety of sizes and colors and usually made of cotton or nylon.

satin: A lustrous, slippery fabric made of silk, rayon, or synthetic fibers. The word *satin* refers to a particular weave structure. Satin ribbon is a commonly available wide-width ribbon.

seersucker: A textured, puckered striped or checked fabric. Seersucker is usually made from cotton or a polyester/cotton blend.

silk: A woven or knit fabric made from a natural protein fiber produced by the silkworm. There are many types of silk, only a handful of which are listed here. Silk takes dye very well and is an insulating fiber.

silk chiffon: A sheer, finely woven, plain-weave fabric that is lightweight and drapes very well. Chiffon may also be made with polyester.

silk organza (organdy): A sheer, finely woven, plain-weave fabric that is lightweight and stiff. Organza may also be made of polyester.

silk shantung: Crisp, plain-weave, textured fabric characterized by the slubs in its silk yarns.

silk taffeta: Crisp, tightly woven, plain-weave fabric.

terrycloth: Woven or knit absorbent fabric with a loop pile on one or both sides. Terrycloth is usually made of cotton or a cotton/polyester blend.

ticking: Medium- to heavyweight cotton, striped fabric. Ticking was originally used for mattresses and pillows.

Ultrasuede: A manmade woven fabric with a velvety nap that is made to look like suede. Ultrasuede is often used for upholstery and is machine washable.

velvet: A densely woven fabric with a short pile on one side. It is available in many types, qualities, and weights. Most velvet is made from silk, rayon, or cotton.

vinyl: A manmade, durable, plastic material available in many different grades and often used when one wants to achieve the look of leather, though vinyl doesn't have the natural fabric's enduring quality. It may or may not be backed with a woven or knit material.

webbing: A very strong fabric, woven in narrow strips and usually made of cotton or nylon, used for harnesses like seatbelts and mountain-climbing gear. Webbing is available in several colors, widths, and strengths. It is sold by the yard at most fabric or trimming stores, as well as at camping and sporting-goods stores.

wool: Woven or knit fabric made with fibers from the fleece of sheep. Like silk, this protein-based material takes dye very well and is a great insulator.

TS FOR SPECIAL OCCASIONS

button scarf

INSPIRED BY THE ELEGANT EVENING STOLE, THIS SCARF IS BOTH STYLISH AND WARM. THOUGH FAUX FUR IS SYNTHETIC AND DURABLE, IT SHOULD BE DRY-CLEANED TO KEEP IT LOOKING LOVELY. FOR A GENTLEMAN'S VERSION, MAKE THE SCARF WITH LAMBSWOOL, CASHMERE, SILK, OR ANY SOFT FABRIC THAT FEELS GOOD AGAINST THE SKIN. TO MAKE A REVERSIBLE SCARF, SEW A BUTTON ON BOTH SIDES. THIS IS A GREAT WAY TO SHOW OFF A BEAUTIFUL ANTIQUE BUTTON YOU LOVE AND ARE WAITING FOR JUST THE RIGHT OPPORTUNITY TO USE.

MATERIALS

¼ yard (22.9cm) faux fur or lambswool, cashmere, etc.

¼ yard (22.9cm) lambswool

Tailor's chalk or fabric marker

Hand-sewing needle

Thimble

Large button, 1" (2.5cm) wide or larger is ideal

INSTRUCTIONS

Cut one 7" × 33" (18 × 83.8cm) piece of faux fur and one 7" × 33" (18 × 83.8cm) piece of lambswool.

Pin the 2 fabrics together with right sides facing. **(A)**

Sew all sides with a ½" (13mm) seam allowance, leaving a 4" (10cm) opening at one end.

Trim the corners, turn right-side out, and push out the corners.

Hand-sew opening closed.

Press the edges on the lambswool side of the scarf with a hot steam iron and press cloth.

Mark the buttonhole on one side of the scarf (whichever fabric is easier to mark) 2" (5cm) from the bottom edge, in the center of the scarf. The buttonhole should be large enough to accommodate the button.

Set the sewing machine to a zigzag stitch and sew a vertical buttonhole (instructions on page 14).

Sew button 4" (10cm) from edge, in the center of scarf. Sew through one fabric layer only. **(B)**

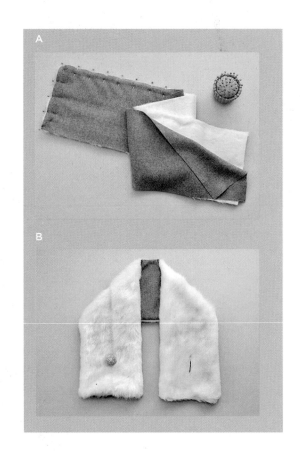

botanical tiara

THESE FLOWERS ARE REALLY VERY SIMPLE TO MAKE, ESPECIALLY FROM ULTRASUEDE, WHICH IS A GREAT NON-FRAYING FABRIC AND IS AVAILABLE IN MANY BEAUTIFUL COLORS, PERFECT FOR FLOWERS. ULTRASUEDE HAS A RIGHT SIDE AND A WRONG SIDE, THOUGH THE DIFFERENCE IS SUBTLE. LOOK CLOSELY AND YOU SHOULD BE ABLE TO DETECT THE NAP. SINCE FLOWERS AND LEAVES ARE ORGANIC OBJECTS, DON'T WORRY ABOUT CUTTING THEM OUT PERFECTLY. USE THE TEMPLATE SIZES AS A GUIDE AND THEN CUT, SEW, AND MIX THE PIECES TOGETHER IN SMALL AND LARGER SIZES. MAKE SOME DIFFERENT SHAPES IF YOU LIKE, TOO. THE ARTIFICIAL STAMENS ARE AVAILABLE AT CRAFT AND FLORAL SUPPLY STORES, BUT YOU COULD CHOOSE TO USE BEADS OR TINY BUTTONS INSTEAD IN THE FLOWER CENTERS. I LIKE TO MAKE A LARGE BATCH OF FLOWERS AND LEAVES, WHICH CAN THEN BE USED TO MAKE TIARAS, CORSAGES, BRACELETS, HAIRCLIPS, AND ADORNMENTS FOR BAGS OR SIMPLY LEFT AS THE BEAUTIFUL OBJECTS THAT THEY ARE.

MATERIALS

1/8 yard (11.4cm) Ultrasuede in different colors (for flowers and leaves)

Fabric marker

Small, sharp scissors

Artificial floral stamens

Hand-sewing needle

Thimble

Wire headband

Stiff paper for templates

Templates, page 114

INSTRUCTIONS

Transfer the templates onto stiff paper. These will be your patterns for tracing onto the fabrics. You may also choose to use the templates as a visual reference only, and cut the leaves and flowers freehand.

TO MAKE FLOWERS

Cut several squares of Ultrasuede slightly larger than the flower patterns. Fold each fabric square in half on the diagonal, right sides together. Sew a seam along the fold, 1/16" (1.6mm) from its folded edge, beginning and ending the stitches 1/4" (6mm) from either end of the fold. Open up the fabric and fold it again, this time on the opposite diagonal, right sides together. Sew a second seam as you did the first, to make an X.

Fold the fabric on the diagonal (one of the sewn seams), right sides together, and trace the template onto the triangle, positioning the straight side of the pattern along the fold. Cut out and open to reveal a flower shape. Refine the shape if needed.

Sew the floral stamens to the center of the flower with one stitch over two stamens. Bend the stamens slightly so they stay vertical.

botanical tiara

TO MAKE LEAVES

Cut several rectangles of Ultrasuede slightly larger than the leaf patterns. Fold each piece of fabric in half lengthwise, right sides together. Sew a seam along the fold, $\frac{1}{16}''$ (1.6mm) from its edge, beginning and ending the stitches $\frac{1}{4}''$ (6mm) from each edge.

With the fabric folded on the sewn seam, trace the template onto the fabric, positioning the straight side along the fold, and cut along the curve. Open to reveal a leaf. **(A)**

TO ATTACH FLOWERS TO HEADBAND

Place a leaf or two under a flower and secure to the wire headband, sewing through all layers.

Start at one end of the headband and, using doubled up and knotted sewing thread, wind thread around the headband several times. Using a thimble (this will make it a lot easier), push the needle up through the wrong side of a leaf and then up through the center of a flower. Push the needle back through both the flower and leaf and wind the thread around the wire headband, attaching both securely.

Add just a flower or just a leaf here and there. Continue sewing flowers and leaves until you are satisfied with the way the tiara looks. **(B)**

tri-pocket ticking tote

TICKING WAS ORIGINALLY A BLUE AND CREAM, VERTICALLY STRIPED WOVEN COTTON USED TO MAKE MATTRESS AND PILLOW CASINGS. TODAY IT IS USED FOR A VARIETY OF APPLICATIONS AND IS AVAILABLE IN MANY COLOR AND STRIPE VARIATIONS, ALL MADE FROM STRONG COTTON CANVAS— THE PERFECT CHOICE FOR A HARDWORKING TOTE BAG. THE SIMPLE PROCESS OF OVERLAPPING THE FABRIC INSTANTLY CREATES THREE POCKETS THAT ARE THE PERFECT SIZE FOR HOLDING A SKETCHBOOK, MAGAZINE, OR LAPTOP. THIS DESIGN IS NARROW ENOUGH THAT IT DOESN'T REALLY NEED POCKET CLOSURES. HOWEVER, IF YOU'D LIKE THEM, ADD SMALL TABS OF VELCRO AT THE TOP CENTER OF EACH POCKET. DEPENDING ON THE SIZE OF YOUR STRIPE, YOU MAY WANT TO CUT SOME OF THE POCKET PIECES LARGER SO YOU CAN LAY OUT OR CENTER THE STRIPES IN THE WAY YOU DESIRE.

MATERIALS

1 yard (91.4cm) striped cotton ticking or canvas, 60" (1.5m) wide

Tailor's chalk or fabric marker

#16 or #18 machine sewing needle

INSTRUCTIONS

TO MAKE THE BAG

Cut two 14" × 19" (35.5 × 48.5cm) pieces of ticking, with the stripes running horizontally along the 14" (35.5cm) edges. Turn and press a large hem on one short edge of each piece. First turn and press a $^1/_4$" (6mm) hem, then turn and press a $2^1/_2$" (6.5cm) hem: This will act as a facing at the opening of the tote. Make sure to turn out this hem (so it lays flat) before pinning and sewing the tote edges. Set aside.

TO MAKE POCKETS

Large pocket: Cut one 14" × 15" (35.5 × 38cm) piece of ticking, with the stripes running vertically down the 15" (38cm) edges.

Medium pocket: Cut one 12" × 14" (30.5 × 35.5cm) piece of ticking, with the stripes running horizontally along the 14" (35.5cm) edges.

Small pocket: Cut one 9" × 14" (23 × 35.5cm) piece of ticking, with the stripes running vertically down the 9" (23cm) edges.

Press and sew a $^1/_4$" (6mm) double hem on one 14" (35.5) side of each of the 3 pocket pieces. **(A)**

tri-pocket ticking tote

With right sides facing up, lay the 3 pockets over the front of one 14" x 19" (35.5 x 49.5cm) bag piece in descending order so they overlap by size (i.e., first place the large pocket, then the medium, then the small). The direction of the stripes will alternate. Match them up at bottom edge. **(B)**

FINISHING THE BAG

Lay the second 14" x 19" (35.5 x 49.5cm) piece of ticking on top of the pockets, right sides facing, and pin around the sides and bottom edges. Make sure to turn out the $2^{1}/_{2}$" (6.5cm) hems that were pressed earlier.

Sew the pinned edges with a $^{1}/_{2}$" (13mm) seam allowance, catching the pocket edges in the side and bottom seams.

Trim the corners, turn right side out, and push out corners. Fold down the $2^{1}/_{2}$" (6.5cm) hem at the top of the bag. **(C)**

TO MAKE HANDLES

Cut two 5" x 25" (12.5 x 63.5cm) strips of ticking, with the stripes running horizontally along the long edge.

Press a $^{1}/_{4}$" (6mm) seam allowance along both long edges of each strip, then press in half lengthwise, wrong sides facing, and secure with pins.

Sew about $^{1}/_{8}$" (3mm) from the edge to close each strip. Sew along the opposite edge as well, also about $^{1}/_{8}$" (3mm) from the edge.

Using tailor's chalk or fabric marker, mark both front and back pieces of the bag on the interior about 2" (5cm) from each side seam and 2" (5cm) below the rim. Pin the handles to the inside of the bag at the marked points.

Sew the handles, making 1" (2.5cm) X boxes at the points of contact. This is important for strength. **(D)**

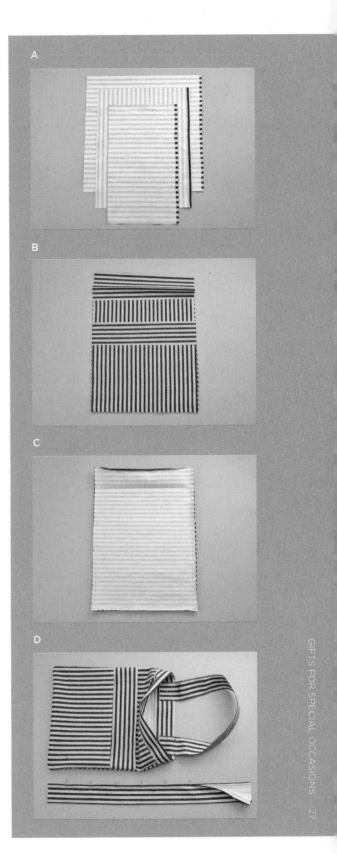

A

B

C

D

ribbon hair clips

SOME RIBBON IS SO GORGEOUS AND CANDY-LIKE THAT YOU JUST HAVE TO HAVE IT. BUT THEN WHAT DO YOU DO WITH THAT MOIRÉ GROSGRAIN FROM FRANCE THAT YOU JUST SPLURGED ON? THE MOST EXQUISITE AND EXPENSIVE RIBBON IS PERFECT FOR THIS PROJECT, SINCE YOU ONLY NEED A SMALL AMOUNT. GO AHEAD AND INDULGE YOURSELF!

MATERIALS

Wide, 9"- (23cm-) long cloth ribbon

Note: A 2"- (5cm-) wide ribbon or wider is ideal; this project uses 3"- (7.5cm-) wide ribbon.

Batting or polyester fiber filling

Metal hairclips, 3" (7.5cm) long

Craft glue (I recommend Gem-Tac glue, available at most craft stores)

INSTRUCTIONS

Fold the ribbon in half crosswise, right sides together, and sew the ends together with a $1/2$" (13mm) seam allowance.

Press the seam open with a warm iron and turn right-side out. You now have a loop.

Flatten the loop and pin one long, open edge of the ribbon together, making sure the seam is in the center. **(A)**

Sew the pinned side of the ribbon.

Stuff the ribbon with a small handful of batting, so it looks like a little pillow.

Pin the other side of the ribbon and sew closed.

Apply a few drops of glue to the metal top of the hairclip and adhere to the back of the ribbon pillow. **(B)**

fanned bag

THIS ELEGANT INDUSTRIAL VENTILATOR BAG IS MADE WITH A MEDIUM-WEIGHT, SLIGHTLY METALLIC VINYL, PRACTICAL FOR A BAG AND IDEAL FOR SHOWING OFF THE SCULPTED PLEATS. IT CAN ALSO BE MADE WITH A SOFT LEATHER OR CANVAS, OR EVEN A HEAVY DUCHESS SILK SATIN. IF YOU WOULD LIKE TO MAKE A LINING FOR THIS BAG, REFER TO THE RICKRACK PURSE, PAGE 40, FOR INSTRUCTIONS. WHEN I GIVE THIS AS A GIFT, I LIKE TO PLEAT IT BACK INTO PLACE SO THAT IT LOOKS LIKE A SIMPLE SQUARE. THEN, WHEN THE RECEIVER OPENS IT UP, THE BAG CAN BE PULLED INTO ITS FANNED SHAPE. I STORE IT AS A SQUARE, TOO, TO KEEP IT LOOKING PERKY AND SCULPTURAL.

MATERIALS

³/₄ yard (68.6cm) medium-weight vinyl

Tailor's chalk

Ruler

INSTRUCTIONS

Cut one 22" × 22" (56 × 56cm) square of vinyl for the bag piece, two 4" × 12" (10 × 30.5cm) rectangles of vinyl for the inside facing pieces, and two 3" × 20" (7.5 × 51cm) strips of vinyl for the bag handles.

Using tailor's chalk, draw 5 pleat lines across the right side of the square piece of vinyl, beginning 3" (7.5cm) from the edge and making each line 4" (10cm) apart. Mark the center points between each pleat line with small marks at both ends. **(A)**

With wrong sides together, fold the vinyl along each pleat line, secure with a few pins, and sew about ¹/₈" (3mm) from the edge of the fold, making little pintucks.

With the pintucks running vertically, fold and pin each pintuck to meet the small center mark, creating a pleat.

Sew pleats into place at both ends, ¹/₄" (6mm) from the edge of the vinyl. These will be the top edges of the bag. **(B)**

Cut two 3" × 20" (7.5 × 51cm) pieces of vinyl for the handles.

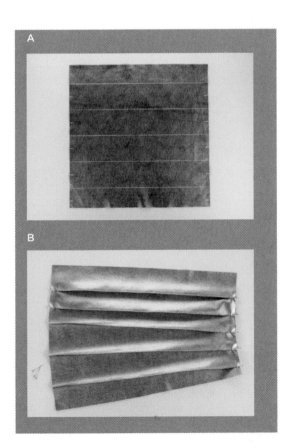

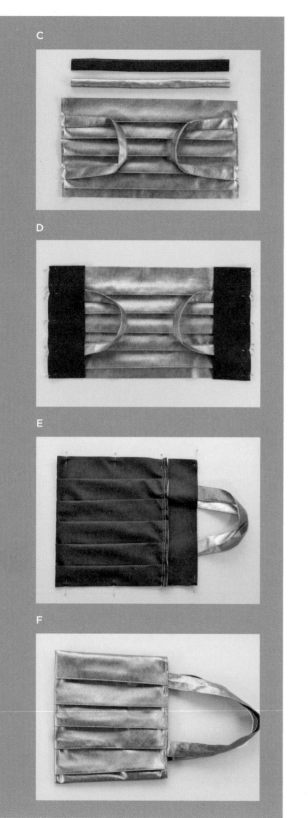

C

D

E

F

fanned bag

Fold in half, right sides together, secure with a few pins, and sew with a $^1/_8$" (3mm) seam allowance. Turn right-side out and sew along each handle edge, sewing as close as possible to the edge.

Pin the ends of the handles to the top (pleated) edge of the bag, about 2" (5cm) from each side seam. **(C)**

Pin each 4" × 12" (10 × 30.5cm) piece of vinyl to each pleated end, over the handles, right sides together. This will be the inside facing of the bag. Sew across each end with a $^1/_2$" (13mm) seam allowance, attaching the handles and the facing at the same time. **(D)**

Fold the pleated piece in half; fold the facing up, right sides together, matching up the facing and the bag seams at each side perfectly.

Pin at this point first, then continue pinning the sides together. The facing should be pinned at the side also. **(E)**

Sew each side of the bag, starting at the facing, with a $^1/_2$" (13mm) seam allowance.

Turn bag right-side out and topstitch along the top edge of the bag with a $^1/_4$" (6mm) seam allowance. **(F)**

Add closures to facing if desired.

ribbon wrap skirt

WRAP SKIRTS AND WRAP DRESSES BECAME POPULAR IN THE '70S AND BOTH CAN NOW BE CONSIDERED CLASSICS. THIS SKIRT IS A GREAT GIFT BECAUSE THE "WRAP" MAKES IT FAIRLY ADJUSTABLE; YOU JUST NEED TO HAVE A GENERAL IDEA OF THE PERSON'S SIZE. THIS PROJECT IS DESIGNED TO BE A MEDIUM BUT SHOULD FIT A VARIETY OF SIZES. IF YOU NEED TO MAKE ADJUSTMENTS, IT'S SIMPLE: CHANGE THE LENGTH FOR A LONGER OR SHORTER SKIRT OR CHANGE THE HORIZONTAL MEASUREMENTS FOR A SMALLER OR LARGER WAIST. SATIN RIBBON MAKES A GOOD WAISTBAND BECAUSE IT IS STIFF ENOUGH TO STAND UP YET DRAPES WELL AFTER IT'S TIED. IT ALSO COMES IN A WIDE VARIETY OF WIDTHS AND COLORS. MAKE SURE TO SELECT POLYESTER SATIN RIBBON SO THE SKIRT WILL BE WASHABLE.

MATERIALS

1½ yards (1.4m) lightweight cotton, 60" (1.5m) wide

3 yards (2.7m) satin ribbon (polyester), 3" (7.5cm) wide

Fabric marker

Fray check

INSTRUCTIONS

This skirt is composed of 3 skirt panels cut on the fold, with the length running along the fold.

For each panel, fold the fabric in half lengthwise, right sides together. With a fabric pen, mark 23" (58.5cm) along the fold for the length, 9" (23cm) from the fold at one end for the waist, and 15" (38cm) from the fold at the opposite end for the hem. Connect the points from the waist to the hem for the side measurement. Cut out skirt panel on the fold, through 2 layers. Each piece when unfolded will measure 18" (45.5cm) wide at waist, 23" (58.5cm) long, and 30" (76cm) wide at the hem.

On the wrong side of each of the 3 skirt panels, mark darts 6" (15cm) long and 1½" (3.8cm) wide. The dart center should be at the middle point of each skirt panel when folded in half. Fold on the center dart line, right sides together, and pin dart in place. **(A)**

Sew all darts, remove pins, and press excess dart fabric toward center of skirt.

With right sides facing, pin the 3 skirt panels together along the lengths, pinning the first to the second, and the second to the third, and sew together with a ¼" (6mm) seam allowance, creating a 3-panel skirt **(B)**

ribbon wrap skirt

Turn, press, and sew $\frac{1}{4}$" (6mm) hems on both 23" (58.5) ends of the 3-panel skirt.

Cut $\frac{1}{2}$"- (13mm-) long slashes into the skirt at the waist: 4 notches on either side of the 2 side seams, about $\frac{1}{2}$" (13mm) apart. The slashes will help the angled fabric ease into the waistband. **(C)**

To make the waistband, fold the 3" (7.5cm) satin ribbon in half lengthwise, wrong sides together. It is important to fold the ribbon perfectly in half. Press with a hot steam iron.

Lay the skirt on a clean, flat surface, right-side up, and carefully pin it into the ribbon waistband, leaving about 38" (96.5cm) of ribbon on the left side of the skirt, and about 25" (63.5cm) of ribbon on the right side. The area at the side seams will need to be eased into the ribbon by lowering the waistline a bit. Pin generously, placing pins about $1\frac{1}{2}$" (3.8cm) apart.

Sew the waistband, with the stitch line about $\frac{1}{8}$" (3mm) from the edge of the ribbon. Make sure to inspect the other side to ensure that the needle is catching the ribbon and the waistband is secured.

Lay the skirt on a clean, flat surface and trim the bottom at the side seams, so that the length is even all the way around.

Turn and press a $\frac{1}{4}$" (6mm) double hem at the bottom of the skirt. **(D)**

Mark a $1\frac{1}{4}$" (3cm) vertical line on the ribbon just above the right side seam and sew a large buttonhole (instructions on page 14). The buttonhole should be long enough for the ribbon to fit through lying flat (pressed in half).

Trim the ribbon ends at 45-degree angles and apply a thin line of fray check.

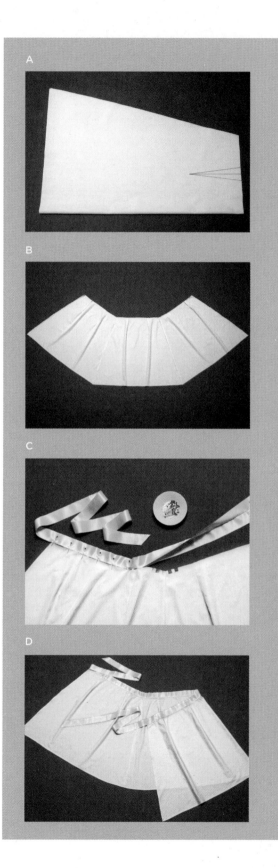

spiral change purse

IT FEELS GREAT TO CREATE SOMETHING SCULPTURAL WITH A SEWING MACHINE. THIS PROJECT
REALLY IS THREE-DIMENSIONAL; WITH SIMPLE CUTTING AND OVERLAPPING OF THE STIFF VINYL, THIS
DESIGN BASICALLY BECOMES A VESSEL. I RECOMMEND USING A FAIRLY STIFF VINYL BECAUSE IT
HOLDS THE SCULPTURAL FORM BETTER. ALSO I RECOMMEND THAT YOU MATCH THE COLOR OF THE
THREAD TO THE VINYL, SO THAT ANY WOBBLY LINES ARE MASKED. THOUGH A ZIGZAG STITCH IS
MORE FORGIVING THAN A STRAIGHT ONE, IT CAN STILL BE TRICKY TO SEW IN A CONTINUOUS
CIRCLE, SO GO SLOWLY.

MATERIALS

$1/4$ yard (22.9cm) medium- to heavyweight,
fabric-backed vinyl

Double-stick tape

One 4" (10cm) length of hook-and-loop
tape (Velcro)

Fabric marker

Small, sharp scissors

Template, page 115

INSTRUCTIONS

Make 2 copies of the spiral template to use as a
paper pattern.

Use double-stick tape to adhere the 2 spiral
patterns to wrong side of vinyl.

Cut out circles and cut out spiral along the solid
lines, using small, sharp scissors. (A)

Remove paper patterns from the vinyl.

Holding the spiral with the right side of fabric in
your palm, push the center point away from
you. Then begin overlapping the spiral from the
inside out, forming a slight cup.

Take note of the direction in which the right
side of the vinyl overlaps, especially at the center. The center point should be on top; the rest
of the vinyl should spiral beneath it. Using the
fabric marker, draw a $1/4$" (6mm) seam allowance line (refer to the dotted line on the
template) along the cut spiral lines. This will
serve as a guide to match to, as the spiral overlaps itself. (B)

Set your sewing machine to a zigzag stitch.
With the wrong side up, start sewing at the
center, overlapping vinyl $1/4$" (6mm) to match
the drawn line guide. Sew very slowly to achieve
the neatest stitch line.

spiral change purse

Repeat with the second spiral.

For the opening of the purse, cut curved pieces of the 4" (10cm) hook-and-loop tape to follow the outside edges of the spiral cup. **(C)**

Place the hook tape along the edge on the wrong side of one spiral cup, and mark the distance with a fabric marker. Do the same to the other spiral cup with the loop tape. This will be the opening of the purse.

Holding the hook-and-loop tape in place, sew the tape to each spiral cup in the areas marked for the opening. If you wish, use tape to keep the hook-and-loop pieces in place.

Place the 2 spirals, wrong sides together, attached at the hook-and-loop area.

If you wish, use tape to hold the 2 spirals together at the unconnected edges and remove as you sew.

Sew the spirals together, starting and stopping at either end of the hook-and-loop opening. **(D)**

Trim the edges if needed, so the two sides match perfectly.

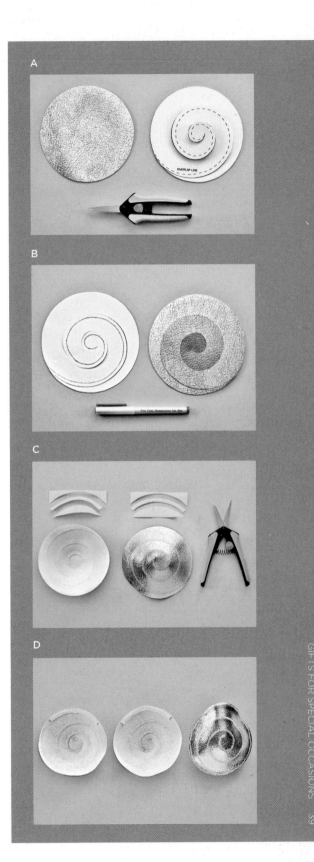

rickrack purse

THIS IS A TRUE TRANSFORMATION PROJECT: A THIN PIECE OF TRIMMING BECOMES AN ELEGANT PURSE FOR A DRESSY AFTERNOON FETE. RICKRACK IS THE CRAFTIEST OF ALL CRAFT MATERIALS, FAMOUS FOR ADORNING APRONS IN THE '40S AND '50S AND FOR DECORATING JUST ABOUT ANYTHING MADE DURING THE CRAFT EXPLOSION OF THE '70S. THIS "MAKE YOUR OWN TEXTILE" PROJECT IS A GOOD EXAMPLE OF HOW YOU CAN TRANSFORM EVEN THE MOST UNLIKELY NOTION INTO AN ELEGANT ACCESSORY—YOU ARE ESSENTIALLY CREATING A LACY FABRIC. WHEN CUTTING THE RICKRACK, BE SURE THAT EACH PIECE IS CUT SYMMETRICALLY—CUT IT AT THE POINTED PART OF THE ZIGZAG SO THAT WHEN THE PIECE IS FOLDED IN HALF CROSSWISE, THE ZIGS AND ZAGS MATCH UP. THIS PROJECT IS SIMPLE IN ITS CONCEPT, BUT BE PREPARED FOR SOME REPETITIVE MACHINE SEWING. IT'S A BIT LIKE AN ASSEMBLY LINE, SO TRY TO RELAX AND EMBRACE THE ZEN OF SEWING. YOU'LL BE AMAZED BY THE STUNNING METAMORPHOSIS.

MATERIALS

11 yards (10m) rickrack, $3/4$"- (2cm-) wide jumbo, cut into thirty-six 9" (23cm) pieces (for the body of the purse) and four 15" (38cm) pieces (for the handles)

$1/4$ yard (22.9cm) silk organza for the lining

Scotch tape, $1/2$" (13mm) wide

INSTRUCTIONS

Arrange 3 of the 9" (23cm) pieces of rickrack lengthwise into groups with the pieces slightly overlapping. Repeat with three more pieces.

Arrange one group of 3 slightly overlapping the other group of 3, positioning them so that the points of the zigzags meet. There should be "holes" created when you arrange them this way. Hold the 6 pieces in place with the tape. Repeat this process to create 6 sections each with 6 pieces of rickrack.

Sew each of the six sections together, stitching crosswise at each end, and at every other point where the rickrack connects (where there is no hole). **(A)**

Arrange the 6 sections so that they slightly overlap one another at the points of the zigzag. There should be more holes created at the joined area. Hold the pieces in place with the tape. Sew the sections together. You will now have a 9" × 14" (23 × 35.5cm) piece of fabric. **(B)**

Fold the rickrack "fabric" in half crosswise, and sew up the sides with a $1/2$" (13mm) seam allowance, avoiding the holes.

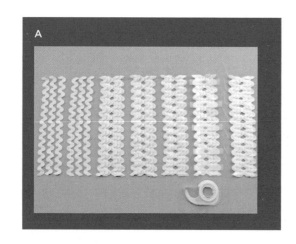

A

TO MAKE THE HANDLES

Place one of the 15″ (38cm) pieces of rickrack on top of a second piece lengthwise, so that the zigzag points alternate. Sew the pieces together down the center. Repeat with the remaining 2 pieces of rickrack.

Pin the handles to the wrong side of the purse, 2″ (5cm) from the side seams. Leave about 1″ (2.5cm) of each end of the handle on the inside of the purse. Repeat on the other side of the purse with the remaining length of rickrack. **(C)**

TO MAKE THE LINING

Cut two 9″ × 9″ (23 × 23cm) squares from the organza. Pin the squares together on 2 opposite sides and sew with a $1/2$″ (13mm) seam allowance.

With wrong sides facing out, slip the lining over the wrong sides of the purse, placing one open end of the organza over the top edges of the purse, overlapping by about 1″ (2.5cm). The side seams of the purse should be aligned with the seams of the lining.

Sew the lining to the purse with the stitch line about $1/2$″ (13mm) from the top edge of the purse. **(D)**

Turn the purse right-side out and away from the lining.

Turn and press a $1/2$″ (13mm) hem on the open end of the lining.

Pin and sew the lining closed, sewing as close to the edge as possible. **(E)**

Push the lining into the purse and press the top seam of the lining to finish.

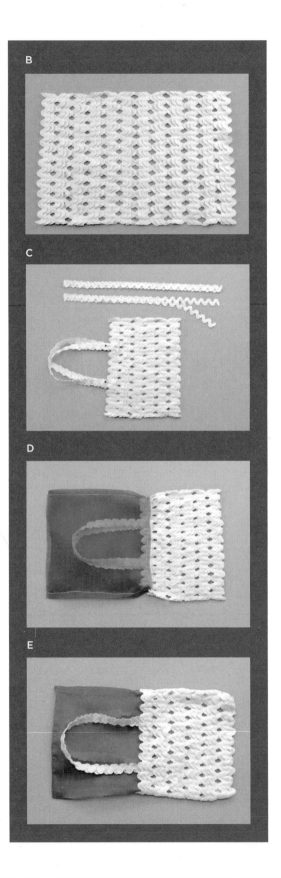

silk loop scarf

THIS PROJECT USES A TECHNIQUE CALLED SLASHED TUCKS. ESSENTIALLY, AFTER SEVERAL IDENTICAL TUCKS ARE SEWN, THEY ARE ALIGNED TOGETHER AND CUT INTO A FRINGE. THE ENDS OF THE FRINGE MAY BE CUT OR REMAIN LOOPED, DEPENDING ON YOUR PREFERENCE. SINCE THE FABRIC IS CUT ON THE BIAS, THE LOOPS WILL BE VERY CLEAN AND CRISP WHEN FRESHLY CUT. OVER TIME, THE LOOP EDGES WILL SOFTEN AND LOSE THAT FRESH-CUT LOOK, FRAYING EVER SO SLIGHTLY, BUT WILL NEVER UNRAVEL. DO NOT PRESS THE LOOPS OR THEY WILL LOSE THEIR PLAYFULNESS.

MATERIALS

1½ yards (1.4m) silk organza
Fabric marker
Long ruler
Small, sharp scissors

INSTRUCTIONS

Press the organza with a hot iron and a press cloth, and lay on a large, flat work surface.

Measure a 15″ x 56″ (38 x 104cm) section on the bias of the organza. It does not have to be a true 45-degree angle.

Mark the scarf measurements with a long ruler.

Turn and press ¼″ (6mm) hems at both short ends.

Four 1″- (2.5cm-) wide tucks (2″ [5cm] of fabric folded in half crosswise) of fabric will be sewn on each end of the scarf, with ½″ (13mm) between each tuck stitch line. Since the tucks should not be pressed and the fabric is stretchy on the bias, it is best to mark the stitch lines before folding the tucks. It doesn't matter which side you mark the lines, as you have the advantage of seeing through the fabric to match the tuck stitch lines together perfectly.

Mark the tuck stitch lines by drawing a line across the scarf width 2″ (5cm) from each short end. This will be the first tuck stitch line, turning the end of the scarf up 1″ (2.5cm) to meet this line.

Mark the additional tuck stitch lines 2″ (5cm) apart, with ½″ (13mm) in between, moving toward the center of the scarf. There should be 7 lines drawn at each end of the scarf. **(A)**

silk loop scarf

Fold over so tuck stitch lines match up through the transparent fabric. Pin and sew along drawn lines. **(B)**

Align the top edges of 4 tucks all together, and pin horizontally across the stitch lines of the tucks.

All 4 stitch lines should be aligned and pinned on top of each other.

Cut through the tucks, starting at one side, every ¼″ (6mm) with a pair of small, sharp scissors. Be careful not to cut too close to the stitch line. Repeat on the other side, cutting the other 4 tucks together. **(C)**

There should be a nice poof of silky loop fringe at each end.

With right sides together, fold in half lengthwise, with the loop fringe on the inside, and pin along the long edge.

Sew with a ¼″ (6mm) seam allowance, stopping at the loop fringe. **(D)**

Turn right-side out.

Press the scarf flat with a hot iron and press cloth.

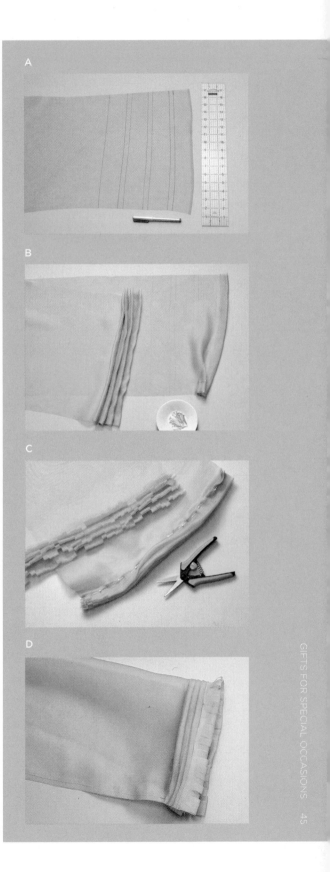

accordion wallet

THIS WALLET IS REALLY QUITE SIMPLE TO MAKE, SO DON'T LET THE VARIOUS STITCH STYLES AND THREAD COLORS—WHICH YOU MUST SWITCH OUT OF YOUR SEWING MACHINE—PUT YOU OFF. YOU CAN MAKE IT SIMPLER BY USING JUST ONE COLOR OF THREAD, IF YOU PREFER. THE SMALL ZIGZAG STITCH PROVIDES A NICE FINISHED LOOK AND IS MORE FORGIVING OF WOBBLY STITCHING. A VINYL FABRIC WITH A SMOOTH SURFACE WILL SEW EASILY WITH A REGULAR PRESSER FOOT. VINYL WITH A SLIGHTLY "STICKY" SURFACE, LIKE A SHINY PATENT-LEATHER FINISH, WILL REQUIRE A PLASTIC PRESSER FOOT. WHEN STRAIGHT-STITCHING, USE AN EXTRA-LONG STITCH TO PREVENT POKING TOO MANY HOLES IN THE VINYL. THE THIN, ADHESIVE-BACKED MAGNETS (USUALLY A ROLL, AVAILABLE AT HARDWARE AND CRAFT STORES) ARE IDEAL FOR THIS WALLET—STRONG ENOUGH TO CLOSE THE WALLET AND LIGHT ENOUGH FOR THE VINYL. SIMPLE SNAPS COULD ALSO BE USED, BUT MAKE SURE TO REINFORCE THEM BY SEWING A SMALL CIRCLE OF VINYL BEHIND EACH SNAP.

MATERIALS

Two $1/4$ yard (22.9cm) pieces of fabric-backed, medium-weight vinyl in different colors

Sewing thread, 2 colors to match the vinyl

Two 1″ x 1″ (2.5 x 2.5cm) magnets cut from a roll of flexible, adhesive-backed magnet tape

Tailor's chalk

INSTRUCTIONS

Cut a $4^1/2$″ x 25″ (11.4 x 63.5cm) strip of vinyl in one color for the compartments of the wallet.

Cut an 8″ x 9″ (20.5 x 23cm) piece of vinyl in the other color for the billfold flap of the wallet. **(A)**

TO MAKE THE COMPARTMENTS

Draw 6 lines on the right side of the long vinyl strip; draw the first line $3^3/4$″ (9.5cm) from one short edge, the next 5 lines $3^1/2$″ (9cm) apart.

Set the sewing machine to a small zigzag stitch (width: 2; length: 1).

Sew a $1/4$″ (6mm) hem on the 2 long sides of the vinyl strip.

Set the machine to a straight stitch.

Fold the strip in half lengthwise, right sides together. Pin one short edge and sew with a $1/4$″ (6mm) seam allowance. Clip the corner and turn right-side out. **(B)**

Press the sewn edge of the strip very lightly with a medium temperature iron and a press cloth, just enough to flatten it out.

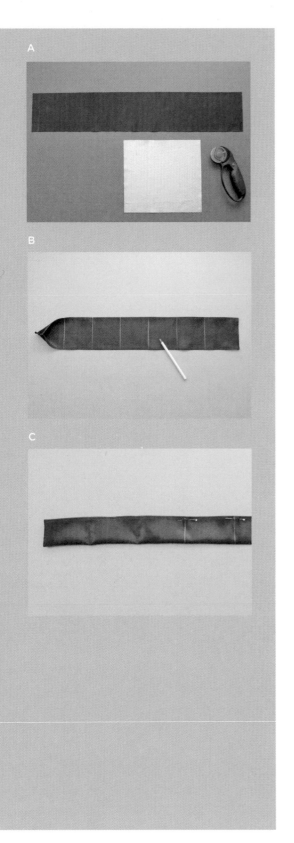

Pin the hemmed edges together, with one pin perpendicular to each drawn line.

Sew along each drawn line (the last compartment should have an open end) to make the compartments. **(C)**

TO MAKE THE FLAP

Change the thread color to match the 8″ × 9″ (20.5 × 23cm) vinyl piece and set machine to zigzag stitch.

Sew a $1/4$″ (6mm) hem on each long edge of the 8″ × 9″ (20.5 × 23cm) vinyl piece.

Set machine to straight stitch.

Fold the vinyl piece in half lengthwise, wrong sides facing, so that hemmed edges meet at the top, and pin the edges. Sew with a $1/4$″ (6mm) seam allowance. Clip the corners and turn right-side out.

Press the sewn edge very lightly with a medium-hot iron and a press cloth.

Set the machine to zigzag stitch and topstitch the three sides of the billfold flap as close as possible to the edge. Do not sew along the hemmed edge.

Align one short edge of the billfold flap perpendicular to one side of the last compartment along the top edge the wallet. Pin top edges together—make sure that the compartment can still be opened. **(D)**

Sew over the topstitching, attaching the billfold flap to the wallet.

Change the thread color to match the wallet and set machine to straight stitch.

Turn the raw edges of the remaining short edge of the wallet to wrong side and sew closed with a $\frac{1}{4}$″ (6mm) seam allowance. **(E)**

Fold up the wallet compartments accordion-style, wrap billfold flap around wallet, and mark for closures. Attach the magnetic closures to the flap at two points: the first centered $1\frac{1}{4}$″ (3cm) from the edge where the flap and wallet are joined and the second on the opposite short edge of the billfold flap, centered $\frac{1}{2}$″ (13mm) from the edge. Make sure they are positioned properly before attaching. **(F)**

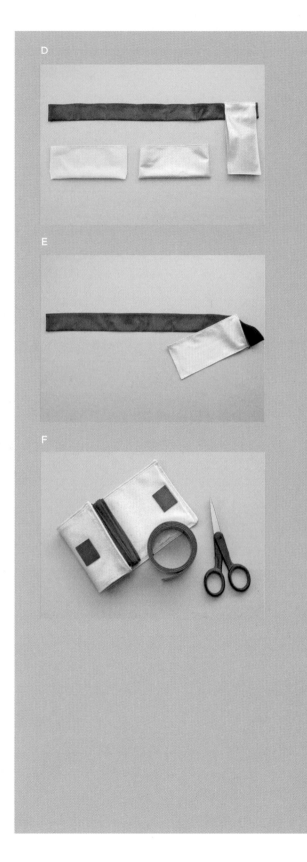

pleated wool scarf

A MEDIUM-WEIGHT WOVEN WOOL IS BEST FOR THIS PROJECT; SINCE IT ONLY REQUIRES ½ YARD (45.7CM), YOU MIGHT WANT TO TRY CASHMERE OR LAMBSWOOL. WHICHEVER FABRIC YOU CHOOSE, IT SHOULD BE OF A WEIGHT SUITABLE FOR A LIGHT WINTER COAT; THE PLEATS WILL HOLD THEIR SHAPE BETTER IF THE FABRIC HAS SOME BODY. ALTER THE WIDTH OR LENGTH OF THE PLEATS IF YOU LIKE, FOR A DIFFERENT EFFECT. OR, TRY PLEATING IN THE OTHER DIRECTION, ACROSS THE WIDTH OF THE SCARF FOR HORIZONTAL PLEATS.

MATERIALS

½ yard (91.4cm) wool, 60" (1.5m) wide

Tailor's chalk

INSTRUCTIONS

Cut a 17" (43cm) piece of wool, from selvedge to selvedge.

Cut off both selvedges.

Press ¼" (6mm) double hems on all sides and sew.

Measure 2" (5cm) from one long edge and draw pleat lines lengthwise, 2" (5cm) apart across the width of the scarf. There should be 7 pleat lines. (Draw lines on right side of the fabric.) **(A)**

Press the pleats, accordion style, with a very hot steam iron. Use a press cloth to prevent scorching. Sew along the length of the pressed pleats, keeping the stitch line about ⅛" (3mm) from the edge. Press again to smooth out the sewn pleats. **(B)**

Fold up accordion style to fit neatly into a gift box.

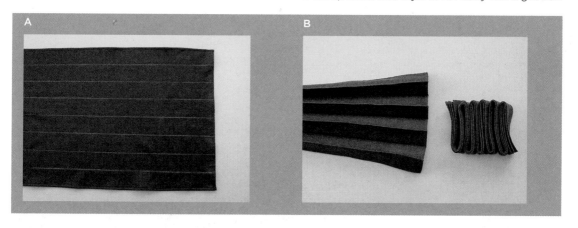

A   B

beaded silk wrap

AN ELEGANT WRAP IS CRUCIAL FOR FORMAL AFFAIRS WHEN A SWEATER OR COAT CLASHES WITH YOUR GOWN. I USE LUXURIOUS SILK SHANTUNG FOR THIS WRAP, BUT YOU CAN CHOOSE ANY ELEGANT, MEDIUM- TO LIGHTWEIGHT FABRIC. SILK COMES IN A WIDE VARIETY OF WEIGHTS AND TEXTURES. SHANTUNG AND TAFFETA, WHICH SHARE SIMILAR WEIGHTS AND DRAPING QUALITIES, WORK VERY WELL FOR THIS WRAP. THE FABRIC WILL LOSE SOME OF ITS STIFFNESS IF IT'S WASHED IN COLD WATER (SHOULD BE AIR DRIED ONLY), AND IT WILL ALSO LOSE SOME OF ITS LUSTROUS SHEEN. TO KEEP IT CRISP, ALWAYS HAVE IT DRY-CLEANED. THE GLASS BEADS HELP TO WEIGH DOWN THE ENDS OF THE WRAP—AND THEY MAKE A COOL SOUND WHEN THEY CLINK TOGETHER!

MATERIALS

2 yards (1.8m) silk (shantung or taffeta)

Note: A 45" (1.1m) width will make exactly 2 wraps

18 glass beads

Note: Choose "pendant" beads, with the hole at the top of the beads, so they can dangle

Fine hand-sewing needle or beading needle (thin enough to pass through the bead holes)

Fabric marker

INSTRUCTIONS

Cut a 21" × 72" (53.5 × 1.8m) piece of silk.

Press $\frac{1}{4}$" (6mm) double hems on all 4 sides of the fabric, using a medium-temperature iron and a press cloth.

Sew $\frac{1}{4}$" (6mm) double hems on all sides of the fabric.

Mark 9 bead points at each short end of the scarf. There should be a bead at each corner, with the other 7 beads spaced about $2\frac{1}{2}$" (6.5cm) apart in between. **(A)**

Hand-sew beads at the points as marked: pass the thread through the bead as many times as you can (2 or 3 times at least) and wind the thread around itself between the bead and the fabric to create a shank. Continue until there are 9 beads at each end. **(B)**

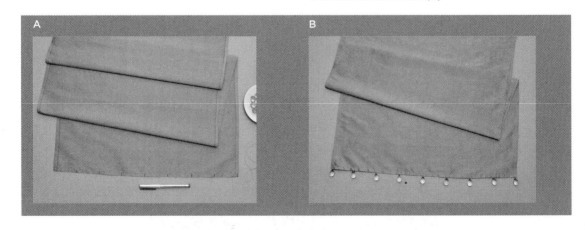

stitched gift wrap

A CLASSIC BROWN PAPER BAG HAS A REALLY GORGEOUS SURFACE. IT'S ALSO STURDY AND AVAILABLE IN A MINUTE TO BECOME FANTASTIC GIFT WRAP. I LOVE THIS PROJECT BECAUSE IT IS SO OPEN TO INTERPRETATION. IT'S AMONG MY FAVORITE RECYCLING PROJECTS BECAUSE YOU CAN USE ANY TYPE OF PAPER, MIX DIFFERENT PAPERS, OR EVEN PATCH PAPERS TOGETHER. I LIKE TO THINK OF IT AS AVANT-GARDE QUILTING.

MATERIALS

Paper bags, different sizes and colors

Paper scraps

Sewing thread, different colors

INSTRUCTIONS

Cut paper bags into square or rectangular pieces.

If you need to, press the paper with a warm iron to remove strong creases.

Set sewing machine to a zigzag stitch.

Sew the paper as you would fabric, embellishing it as desired, using a variety of stitches and thread colors. **(A)**

To make a large piece of gift wrap, sew sections together, randomly or in a pattern. Continue sewing until the paper is large enough to wrap your gift.

Sew several long strips to make a ribbon, or cut strips from stitched paper and form loops to create a decorative bow. **(B)**

A

B

TS FOR THE HOME

fringed sachets

HANDKERCHIEF LINEN IS A FINE, LIGHTWEIGHT FABRIC WITH A SLIGHT TRANSLUCENCE THAT IS PERFECT FOR ALLOWING THE FRAGRANT SCENT OF LAVENDER TO FLOW THROUGH. FIND A NICE COLOR COMBINATION AND MAKE MANY AT ONCE. I LIKE TO GIVE A SET OF FIVE OR SIX SACHETS, STACKED UP IN A LITTLE BOX. GIVE THE FRINGE A GOOD PRESS WITH A HOT IRON BEFORE YOU WRAP THEM UP.

MATERIALS

$^1/_8$ yard (11.4cm) handkerchief or other thin linen, in two different colors

Note: A 45" (1.1m) width will make 11 sachets

Lavender, 2 tablespoons per sachet

INSTRUCTIONS

Cut two 4" (10cm) strips from selvedge to selvedge, one of each color of linen.

Cut carefully, so that the grain of the fabric aligns with the cut line. This is important for an even fringe. **(A)**

Cut the strips into 4" x 4" (10 x 10cm) squares.

Place 2 squares together, pin and sew on 3 sides with a $^3/_4$" (2cm) seam allowance.

Fill with 2 tablespoons of lavender.

Sew remaining side closed.

Fringe by gently pulling away threads from the edges, until there is about $^1/_4$" (6mm) of fringe. **(B)**

Repeat the process to make as many as you like.

Press fringe on each finished sachet for a clean look.

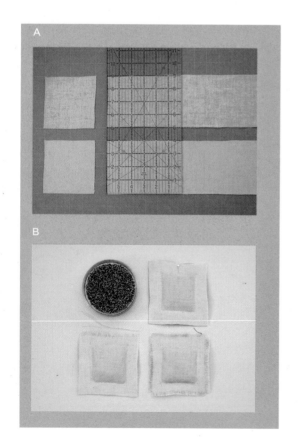

speckle pillow

DOTTED SWISS WAS A POPULAR CURTAIN FABRIC IN THE EARLY HALF OF THE TWENTIETH CENTURY, PRIZED FOR ITS SHEERNESS. IT WAS ALSO A FAVORITE CHOICE AMONG DRESSMAKERS, SINCE THE UNIFORM DOTS MADE A PERFECT GRID FOR SMOCKING. THOUGH IT IS AVAILABLE IN SEVERAL SHADES TODAY, WHITE IS STILL THE MOST COMMON. WHITE IS ALWAYS MY CHOICE FOR BED SHEETS, AND THESE PILLOWS ARE PERFECT TO BE PAIRED WITH CRISP, COTTON SHEETS. DOTTED SWISS IS SOFT AND TEXTURAL, AND WHEN LAYERED OVER POLKA DOTS IT CREATES A COOL DOTTED EFFECT.

MATERIALS

1 yard (91.4cm) polka-dot print, 45" (1.1m) wide

1/2 yard (45.7cm) cotton dotted swiss, 54" (1.4m) wide

Pillow form, 14" x 18" (35.5 x 45.5cm)

INSTRUCTIONS

Cut the polka-dot print into 3 pieces: one 18" x 22" (45.5 x 56cm) piece for the front of the pillowcase and two 18" x 14" (45.5 x 35.5cm) pieces for the back of the pillowcase.

Cut the dotted swiss into 3 pieces: one 18" x 22" (45.5 x 56cm) piece for the front of pillowcase and two 18" x 14" (45.5 x 35.5cm) pieces for the back of the pillowcase.

Lay one back piece of the polka-dot print over one back piece of dotted swiss, wrong sides facing up. Press 1/4" (6mm) double hem on one 14" (35.5cm) edge (or, if using another size pillow, one long edge of the fabric). Secure the pressed hem with pins and sew.

Repeat for the other back piece.

Lay the front piece of the dotted swiss over the front piece of the polka-dot print, right sides facing up.

Lay the 2 back pieces on top of the front piece, right sides together. There should be a 4" (10cm) vertical overlap in the center. **(A)**

Pin all edges and sew with a 1/4" (6mm) seam allowance. Trim the corners, turn right-side out, and push out the corners.

Sew a flange by topstitching all the way around the edges, with a 1" (2.5cm) seam allowance. **(B)**

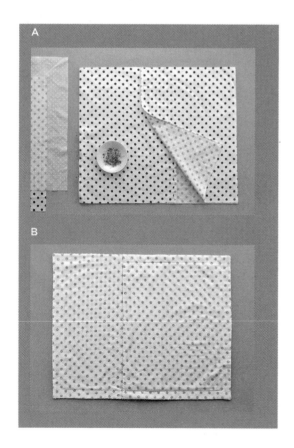

shirred pillow

VELVET IS A LUMINOUS, PLUSH MATERIAL. WHEN USED FOR SOMETHING SMALL LIKE A PILLOW, IT CAN GLOW LIKE A GEM. SHIRRING IS A GREAT TECHNIQUE TO USE WITH VELVET BECAUSE THE DIMENSION CREATED BY THE GATHERS ENHANCES THE FABRIC'S QUALITIES EVEN MORE. WHEN GIVING IT AS A GIFT, MAKE SURE YOU KNOW THE RECIPIENT'S COLOR PREFERENCE, AND WHEN IN DOUBT, USE A NEUTRAL SHADE. IT'S BEST TO USE A MEDIUM-WEIGHT VELVET; IT CAN BE DIFFICULT TO WORK WITH ANYTHING LIGHTER, ESPECIALLY WHEN YOU ARE TRYING TO PIN THE SHIRRED PIECE TO THE FLAT PIECE. THIS PART TAKES A LITTLE PATIENCE AND A LOT OF PINS TO MAKE SURE IT ALL GETS ATTACHED. AFTER THAT, IT'S SIMPLE.

MATERIALS

³/₄ yard (68.6cm) medium-weight velvet, cotton, silk, or rayon

Tailor's chalk or fabric marker

Ruler, 24" (61cm) or longer

Hand-sewing needle

Pillow form, 12" × 22" (30.5 × 56cm)

INSTRUCTIONS

It is important to first decide the direction of the shirring in order to know how much fabric you will need and how to cut it. After you measure the pillow, double the length for the direction of the shirring.

Cut one 13" × 23" (33 × 58.5cm) piece of fabric for the pillow back (the same dimensions as the pillow form plus a 1" [2.5cm] seam allowance). Cut a 26" × 23" (66 × 58.5cm) piece of fabric for the pillow front. It will be double the length of the back to accommodate the shirring.

Decide on the number of shirred stitching lines. To make 8, use a long ruler and tailor's chalk or a fabric marker to mark the lines across the wrong side of the front piece. Space the lines evenly across the fabric, working out from the center, about 2" (5cm) apart.

Set the sewing machine to the longest stitch possible and sew along the lines, without backtacking at the beginning or the end. Leave at least 6" (15cm) thread tails at both ends. **(A)**

Gather the fabric by pulling on the threads. Gather half the fabric from one thread end and half from the other thread end. Continue until all threads have been pulled and the gathered fabric matches the dimensions of the back piece.

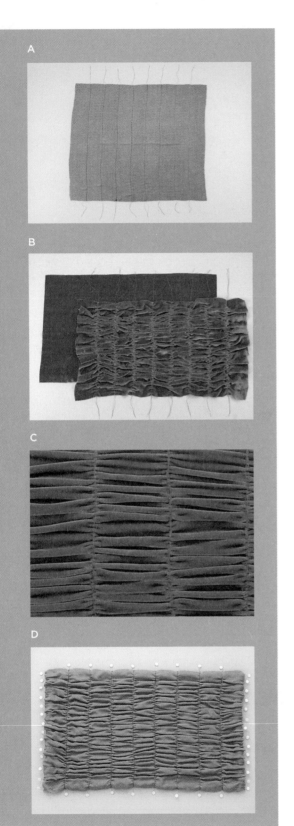

A

B

C

D

Move the gathers around until the shirring looks even, then knot both thread ends to keep the lengths in place, and trim excess thread. **(B)**

Set the sewing machine to a short stitch and sew over the original shirred stitch lines on the right side of the fabric. Keep the original stitch line in view by pulling the shirred fabric horizontally, as you sew. The shirring should now be stabilized. **(C)**

Pin the shirred piece and the flat piece, right sides together. Use a generous amount of pins to tack all the excess fabric down on the sides before stitching. **(D)**

Begin sewing on a side that has shirred ends, sewing all the way around, with a $1/2''$ (13mm) seam allowance. Leave an opening large enough to insert the pillow, about 12" (30.5cm).

Trim the corners, turn right-side out, and push out the corners.

Insert the pillow form into the case.

Hand-sew the opening closed.

wave place mats

THESE PLACE MATS ARE SIMILAR TO THE PINTUCKED TABLE RUNNER (PAGE 68) AND, IF YOU'RE REALLY AMBITIOUS, MAKE A NICE COMPANION GIFT TO IT. HERE, I USE COTTON CANVAS RATHER THAN LINEN. IT'S STIFFER, AND ITS HEAVIER WEIGHT MAKES THE WAVES STAND UP NICELY, PROVIDING A MORE SCULPTURAL EFFECT.

MATERIALS

Cotton canvas, 45" (1.1m) wide:
1 yard (91.4cm) for 4

1 yard (91.4cm) medium-weight cotton, for underlining

Rayon sewing thread in a contrasting color

Fabric marker or tailor's chalk

Ruler

Hand-sewing needle

INSTRUCTIONS

TO MAKE 4 PLACE MATS

Cut cotton canvas to measure 30" × 44" (76.2 × 112cm). Cut 4 pieces of cotton underlining, each measuring 15" × 21" (38 × 53.5cm).

On a flat work surface, use a ruler to draw lines dividing the canvas into 4 quarters, each measuring 15" × 22" (38 × 56cm). Each section represents a placemat.

Draw 4 lines 1" (2.5cm) apart at the edge of each place mat. (A)

These lines will be small pleats, or pintucks.

Use an iron to press the pintucks into place by folding the fabric, wrong sides together, on the drawn lines. Sew the pintucks into place with a contrasting color rayon thread, with the stitch line 1/8" (3mm) from the edge of the fold.

Cut the cotton canvas on the marked lines for 4 place mat pieces, and press out the pleats.

To create the wave effect, mark each place mat with 3 short horizontal lines across the place mat and over the pintucks. Each line will push the pleats to one side or the other so that the pleats fall in alternate directions. Draw the first line 4" (10cm) up from the bottom, the next 2 lines 3 1/2" (9cm) apart. (B)

Change the thread to match the canvas color.

Press the pleats, pushing them with your hand in alternating directions, and sew along the drawn lines to secure the pintuck waves.

Pin the canvas and the cotton underlining with right sides together, sew all sides with a $1/2''$ (13mm) seam allowance, and leave a 3" (7.5cm) opening.

Trim the corners, turn right-side out, and push out the corners. Press the edges of the place mat and the pleated waves and hand-sew the opening closed.

pintucked table runner

PINTUCKING IS A SUPER SIMPLE AND BEAUTIFUL TECHNIQUE THAT ALLOWS YOU TO CREATE TEXTURE ON AN OTHERWISE SMOOTH SURFACE. WHEN YOU SEW THE PINTUCKS WITH SHINY, COLORFUL THREAD, YOU ADD EVEN MORE VISUAL INTEREST TO THE NEWLY TEXTURED PIECE OF FABRIC, ESPECIALLY WHEN IT IS AS EXPANSIVE AS A TABLE RUNNER. THE VERSATILITY OF A TABLE RUNNER IS SO APPEALING; MAKE IT NARROW OR WIDE AND VARY THE LENGTH AS YOU DESIRE.

MATERIALS

Linen, top fabric, length and width based on table, with $1/4$" (6mm) added to length for each pintuck

Lightweight fabric, sized to match top fabric

Fabric marker or tailor's chalk

Ruler

Rayon sewing thread in a contrasting color

Hand-sewing needle

INSTRUCTIONS

Decide on the finished length and width of the table runner. Decide on the number of pintucks. Add $1/4$" (6mm) for each pintuck to the length measurement. To determine cutting size, add $1/2$" (13mm) seam allowance on all sides.

Cut linen piece and use the ruler to draw lines across the width of the right side of the linen in a random pattern for pintuck placement. (A)

Press the pintucks into place by folding the fabric, wrong sides together, on the drawn lines

Sew the pintucks into place with rayon thread of a contrasting color. The stitch line should be $1/8$" (3mm) from the edge of the fold.

Iron the pintucked linen piece so that the pleats are pressed in the same direction and the piece is pressed out as flat and straight as possible. (B)

Measure the pintucked linen and cut underlining fabric to match.

Pin the pintucked linen and muslin with right sides together, and sew with a $1/2$" (13mm) seam allowance, leaving a 6" (15cm) opening at one end.

Trim corners, turn right-side out, and push out the corners. Press entire runner and hand-sew the opening closed.

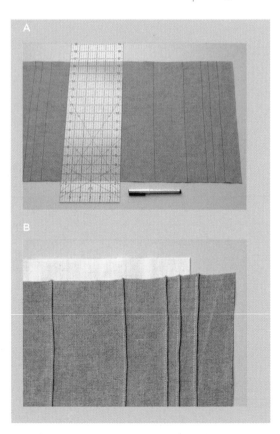

shirting stripe duvet cover

THE CHANCES OF A STORE-BOUGHT DUVET COVER FITTING A COMFORTER PERFECTLY ARE SLIM. THIS IS WHERE THE HANDMADE TRUMPS THE MANUFACTURED! IF POSSIBLE, SNEAK INTO THE BEDROOM OF YOUR PROSPECTIVE GIFT RECIPIENT AND MEASURE THE TARGETED COMFORTER. TAKE NOTE OF THE BEDROOM COLORS AND DÉCOR WHILE YOU'RE AT IT. THIS DUVET COVER CALLS FOR 45"- (1.1M-) WIDE FABRICS, SO IF YOU NEED TO MAKE A LARGER DUVET COVER, PURCHASE 60" (1.5M) WIDTHS. SHIRTING FABRIC TENDS TO BE NICE, CRISP WOVEN COTTON, MUCH FINER THAN A TYPICAL COTTON PRINT. WHEN MAKING SOMETHING LARGE LIKE A DUVET, YOU ALMOST ALWAYS NEED TO SEW WIDTHS OF FABRIC TOGETHER AND THE STRIPES CONVENIENTLY SERVE AS A SEWING GUIDE. FOR THE BACK SIDE, I USED A SOLID, LESS EXPENSIVE COTTON BROADCLOTH, WHICH IS AVAILABLE IN A VARIETY OF COLORS SO THAT YOU CAN EASILY COMPLEMENT THE SHIRTING STRIPE. THIS DUVET COVER WOULD ALSO BE GORGEOUS MADE IN DIFFERENT COLORS OF LINEN AND COTTON. THE BUTTONS ARE MADE WITH A COVERED BUTTON KIT, AVAILABLE AT ALL SEWING STORES.

MATERIALS

For a Full/Queen size comforter measuring 84" × 84" (2.1 × 2.1m) or smaller:

Two 2½ yards (2.3m) cotton shirting stripe in 2 different colors/designs, 45" (1.1m)wide, with stripes running vertically up the bolt of fabric

5 yards (4.6m) cotton broadcloth of a solid color, 47" (1.2m) wide

Fabric marker

2 buttons, ¾" (2cm) in diameter

Hand-sewing needle

Note: This finished duvet cover measures 84½" (2.1m) wide by 84¼" (2.1m) long

INSTRUCTIONS

TO MAKE THE FRONT OF THE DUVET

Cut one 2½ yard (2.3m) piece of shirting stripe in half lengthwise, with each half measuring 22½" × 85" (57.2 × 216cm). These 2 pieces will be sewn to either side of the other shirting stripe, creating the front of the duvet cover.

Cut the second striped fabric to measure 43" × 85" (109 × 216cm).

Pin one of the narrow shirting stripe pieces to either long edge of the wide piece, right sides together, and sew with a ¼" (6mm) seam allowance. Press seams open.

Turn and press a 1" (2.5cm) hem on one width edge (along the stripes) of the front piece. This will be the bottom seam, where the buttonhole is stitched. (A)

TO MAKE THE BACK OF THE DUVET

Cut the cotton broadcloth into 2 pieces, each measuring 47" × 85" (119 × 216cm).

With right sides together, pin together along the long edges, and sew with a ¼" (6mm) seam allowance. Press seam open.

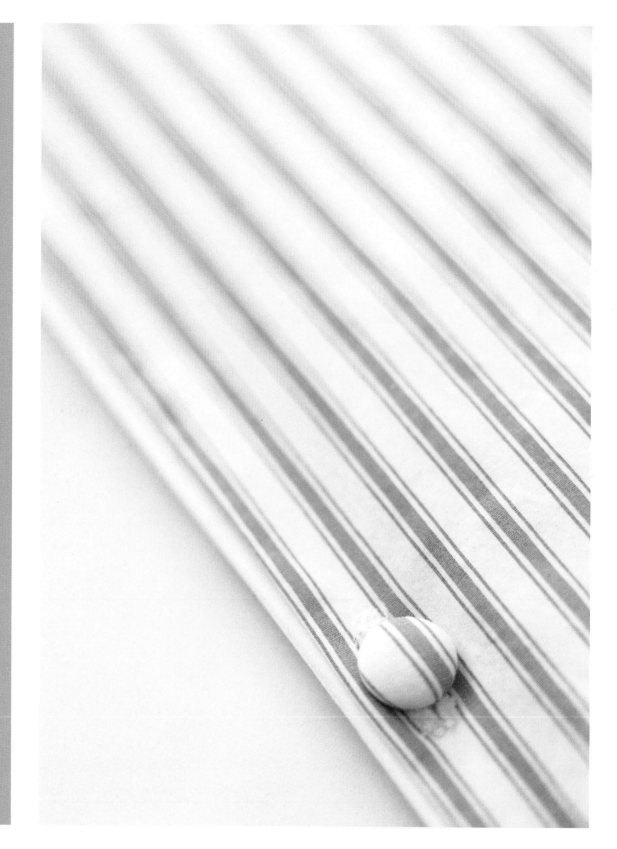

shirting stripe duvet cover

Turn, press, and sew a 1/4" (6mm) double hem on one wide edge (this is the bottom edge).

On a clean, smooth surface, lay out the striped front piece, right-side up. (The 1" [2.5cm] pressed hem on the striped piece should be considered the bottom edge.)

Aligning the top edges, carefully place the solid back piece over the front piece, right sides together. The bottom edge has the sewn hem. Carefully align the sides and smooth out the fabrics. At the bottom, there will be about 7" (18cm) extra on the back piece. Fold this extra fabric up so the bottom edges of the front and back pieces are equal in length, and pin in place. This is the small pocket for the comforter. **(B)**

Mark a 24" (61cm) opening at the center bottom of the fabrics. Begin pinning at the opening and pin all the way around, stopping at the other end of the opening. More pins make it easier to keep the fabrics straight and aligned when sewing.

Sew the bottom edge with a 1" (2.5cm) seam allowance. Sew the other 3 sides with a 1/4" (6mm) seam allowance. **(C)**

Turn right-side out (no need to trim the corners here) and push out the corners.

Press bottom edge, making sure that the 1" (2.5cm) seam allowance at the opening is completely flush with the rest of the sewn edge. This will serve as the placket for the buttons and buttonholes.

Mark 2³/4" (7cm) diameter buttonholes on the striped fabric, each 8" (20.5cm) from the ends of the opening. **(D)**

Sew buttonholes (instructions on page 14).

Hand-sew buttons to the 1" (2.5cm) seam allowance on the fabric opposite the buttonhole.

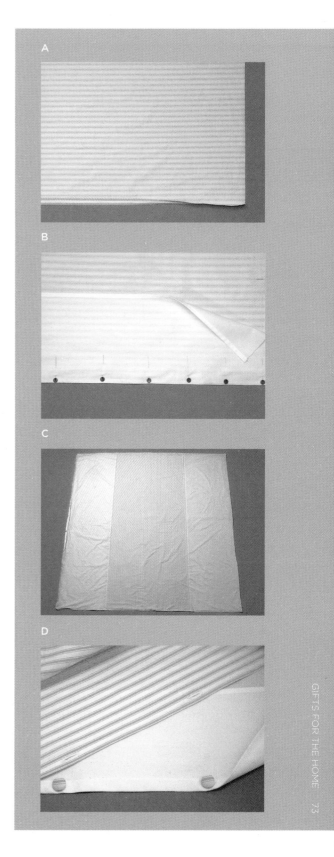

luxurious throw

EVERYONE LOVES A GIFT MADE WITH CASHMERE, THE PINNACLE OF TEXTILE LUXURY. COMBED FROM THE BELLIES OF GOATS IN THE MOUNTAINOUS REGIONS OF ASIA, CASHMERE HAS A SOFTNESS THAT IS UNRIVALED. THE SIMPLE EDGING OF CASHMERE TURNS THIS WOOL BLANKET INTO A SUMPTUOUS THROW. IF YOU LOOK AT ANY QUILTING BOOK, YOU WILL SEE THAT MOST BINDING IS MACHINE-STITCHED ON ONE SIDE AND HAND-STITCHED ON THE OTHER SIDE. THIS PROJECT USES AN UNCONVENTIONAL BINDING METHOD THAT IS ALL DONE ON THE SEWING MACHINE. THE USE OF A ZIGZAG STITCH HERE IS INSTRUMENTAL IN HELPING TO CATCH THE OTHER SIDE, BUT THE FIRST PRIORITY SHOULD BE TO PIN AS PLENTIFULLY AND PERFECTLY AS POSSIBLE. QUILTING PINS ARE RECOMMENDED BECAUSE THEY ARE LONGER THAN REGULAR PINS AND WILL MAKE PINNING THE LAYERS TOGETHER A LOT EASIER.

MATERIALS

1½ yards (1.4m) lambswool, 60" (152cm) wide

1 yard (91.4cm) lightweight cashmere, 60" (152cm) wide

Fabric marker

Ruler, 24" (61cm) clear ruler is ideal

Quilting pins

INSTRUCTIONS

TO MAKE THE BINDING

Cut four 9"- (23cm-) wide strips of cashmere across the fabric, from selvedge to selvedge.

Using a ruler and a fabric marker, draw a ½" (13mm) seam allowance on both long edges of all 4 strips. Turn and press with a hot steam iron and press cloth.

Fold each of the four strips in half lengthwise, wrong sides together, and press with a hot steam iron. These pieces are going to bind the blanket with 4"- (10cm-) wide edges of cashmere.

Each binding strip should be 1½" (3.8cm) longer than the side of the blanket it will bind. For this blanket, 2 strips will be 55½" (141cm) long and 2 strips will be 60" (152cm) long.

Trim the ends of the binding pieces at 45-degree angles. A cutting mat with 45-degree-angle lines is especially helpful here. The longer side should be the folded (outer) edge, and the shorter side should be the open (inner) edge. **(A)**

To create the binding "frame," open the binding pieces and pin the ends of one short piece to one long piece, right sides together, forming a mitered corner. Place first pin at the very center.

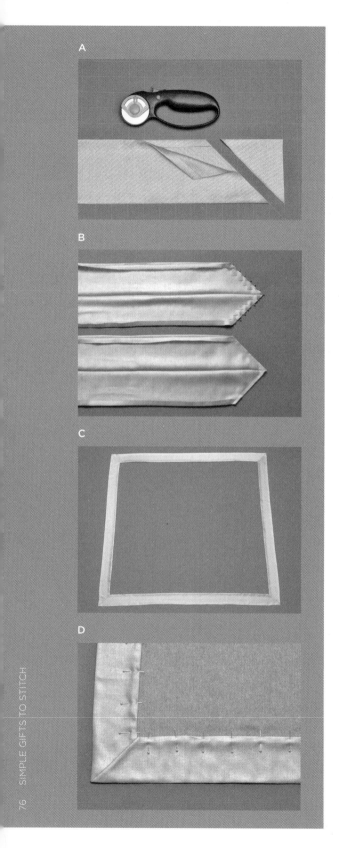

A

B

C

D

luxurious throw

Align the points perfectly, and then pin the edges, aligning the ends perfectly. Place several pins in between, about $\frac{1}{2}$" (13mm) apart, and sew with a $\frac{1}{4}$" (6mm) seam allowance. **(B)**

Sew the 4 binding pieces together in this way. Trim corners and turn right-side out. You should now have what resembles a frame, with the 4 pieces of cashmere binding connected with mitered corners.

Press the corners flat with a hot steam iron and press cloth. **(C)**

TO MAKE THE BLANKET

Cut a lambswool piece to measure 54" × 58$\frac{1}{2}$" (137 × 149cm).

Lay the lambswool on a clean, flat surface and place the binding over it, aligning the short sides and long sides.

Gradually place the lambswool inside the binding, shifting and straightening the two as you go. There should be about $\frac{1}{2}$" (13mm) of extra space between the blanket edge and the binding edge. This allows for some variation, so some areas may have $\frac{1}{4}$" (6mm), etc. The most important thing is to keep the blanket looking straight and square.

Once the blanket is placed inside the binding, start pinning. It is very important to make sure the two sides of the binding are aligned perfectly, so that the stitch catches the other side of the binding. You should be able to feel the inner edge of the binding through the blanket with your hands as you pin. The more you pin, the easier it will be, so pin about every inch. **(D)**

Set the sewing machine to the widest zigzag stitch. Test the stitch on a fabric scrap first. Starting at one corner, topstitch all sides with the zigzag stitch close to the inner edge of the binding. Periodically check the other side to ensure that the zigzag stitch is sewing the binding properly.

modern apron

SEERSUCKER WAS VERY POPULAR IN THE '30S AS A MEN'S SUITING FABRIC. IT HAS A CASUAL ELEGANCE, IS EASY TO CARE FOR, AND DOESN'T WRINKLE MUCH. CUT ON THE BIAS, AS IT IS HERE, IT TAKES ON A MORE MODERN LOOK. COTTON SEERSUCKER IS VERY LIGHTWEIGHT BUT STRONG AND ABSORBENT—PERFECT FOR AN APRON! I LIKE TO EXPERIMENT WITH CLEVER WAYS TO PACKAGE THINGS, AND THIS PARTICULAR PROJECT FOLDS UP NICELY INTO A GIFT BOX.

MATERIALS

1 yard (91.4cm) striped seersucker fabric, 58" (147cm) wide

Yardstick or long ruler (helpful but not necessary)

Fabric marker

Measuring guide, page 116

INSTRUCTIONS

Lay the seersucker on a flat, clean surface with the stripes running vertically.

Cut off the selvedge on one edge, then cut 2 vertical strips, each measuring $4\frac{1}{2}$" × 36" (11.4 × 91.4cm), or longer if needed or desired. These will be the apron ties.

Hold the upper-right-hand corner of the remaining fabric and fold down diagonally, toward the lower-left corner, so that the corner reaches about 8" (20.5cm) past the bottom edge of the fabric. The apron will be cut on this diagonal fold.

Following the measuring guide, mark the dimensions of the apron on the fabric. Position the center front of the apron along the fold. The seersucker stripes will run diagonally across the apron. Use pins to keep the fabric from shifting on the fold, and make sure that both layers of fabric are cut on these drawn lines as well. **(A)**

Cut out the apron on the drawn lines through both layers of the fabric. Press a $\frac{1}{2}$" (13mm) double hem on all edges of the apron.

With right sides together, fold the 2 apron ties in half lengthwise and press lightly.

Sew the raw edges of the 2 apron ties with a $\frac{1}{4}$" (6mm) seam allowance and turn right-side out. Press flat.

modern apron

Turn one end in with a $1/4''$ (6mm) hem and press. Sew the end closed by stitching as close as possible to the edge.

Pin the apron ties to either side of the apron waist, tucking the raw edge of the ties into the apron's $1/2''$ (13mm) hems. **(B)**

Cut a vertical strip, along the bias, measuring $2 1/2'' \times 23''$ (6.5 × 58.5cm). This will be the neck strap.

Press a $3/8''$ (9.5mm) hem on both sides of the neck strap. Fold in half lengthwise, wrong sides together, and press again.

Sew the long edge of the neck strap closed, stitching as close as possible to the edge. Sew the opposite side the same way. **(C)**

Pin the neck strap to either side of the apron bib, tucking the raw edges of the strap into the apron's $1/2''$ (13mm) double hems. By doing this, both the neck strap and the ties will be stitched on as the apron is hemmed.

Sew a $1/2''$ (13mm) double hem on all sides of the apron.

Sew a second row of stitching $3/8''$ (9.5mm) from the first row of stitching at the top of the bib, to further secure the neck strap. **(D)**

Sew a second row of stitching at the apron ties, again to further secure them in place.

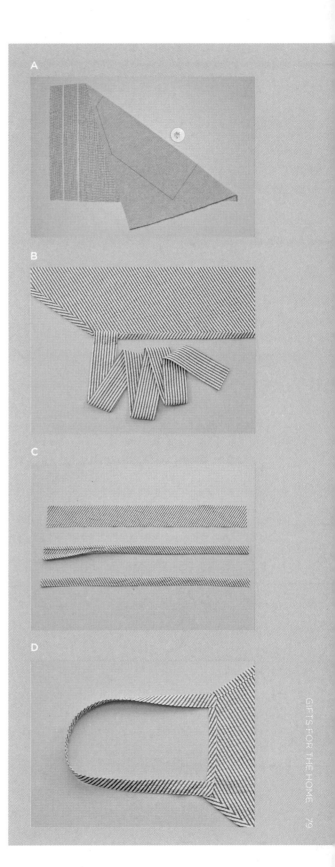

A

B

C

D

pulled-thread coasters

THE PULLED-AND-DRAWN THREAD TECHNIQUE IS ALMOST A LOST ART, AS ARE MANY HAND NEEDLEWORK TECHNIQUES. AUTHENTIC PULLED-AND-DRAWN THREAD PROJECTS INVOLVE MUCH MORE THAN SIMPLY PULLING THREADS OUT, BUT THIS PROJECT DISTILLS IT DOWN TO JUST THAT. THE TWO COLORS THAT CREATE A CHAMBRAY ARE REALLY SHOWCASED HERE. IT'S EXCITING TO SEE THE WARP AND WEFT COLORS REVEAL THEMSELVES AS STRIPES. THE CONTRASTING COLOR COTTON THAT POPS THROUGH THE LITTLE SQUARE ADDS ANOTHER ELEMENT OF SURPRISE.

MATERIALS

$^{1}/_{2}$ yard (45.7cm) linen chambray

Note: A 10″ × 15″ (25.5 × 38cm) piece will make 6 coasters

$^{1}/_{2}$ yard (45.7cm) medium-weight cotton in a contrasting color to linen

Seam ripper

Fabric marker

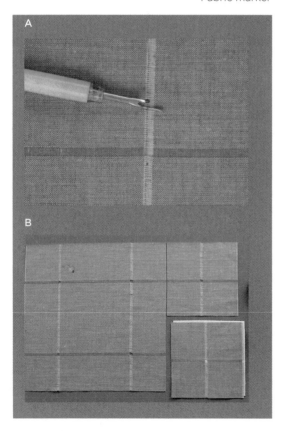

INSTRUCTIONS

Cut a 10″ × 15″ (25.5 × 38cm) piece of linen. Cut carefully so that the grain of the fabric aligns with the cut line. This is so that the pulled-thread design will be centered on the coaster.

Mark the pulled-thread designs by drawing 3 vertical lines on the linen at 2$^{1}/_{2}$″, 7$^{1}/_{2}$″, and 12$^{1}/_{2}$″ (6.5cm, 19cm, and 30.5cm).

Draw 2 horizontal lines at 2$^{1}/_{2}$″ and 7$^{1}/_{2}$″ (6.5cm and 19cm).

Start pulling threads at each line using a seam ripper; carefully pull up one individual thread to start the line. Once the first thread is pulled out, it gets easier to pull the rest. The stripes on these coasters are about $^{1}/_{4}$″ (6mm) wide. Continue pulling at each drawn line until you are satisfied with the design. **(A)**

Cut the linen and the cotton into 6 squares, each measuring 5″ × 5″ (12.5 × 12.5cm). **(B)**

Pin the linen and cotton (right sides facing, if fabrics have a right side) and sew all sides with a $^{1}/_{2}$″ (13mm) seam allowance, leaving a 2″ (5cm) opening.

Trim the corners, turn right-side out, and push out the corners. Press with a hot steam iron and a press cloth. Hand-sew the opening closed.

button-stitch dishtowels

THESE WERE INSPIRED BY MY THREE FAVORITE DISHTOWELS, MADE IN FRANCE, EACH ONE A
DIFFERENT COLOR IN A SIMPLE PLAID. A MEDIUM-WEIGHT LINEN/COTTON BLEND IS AN EXCELLENT
CHOICE FOR A DISHTOWEL BECAUSE LINEN IS SUPER STRONG AND COTTON IS VERY ABSORBENT.
THE BUTTONHOLE MAKES THESE UNIQUE. MOST DISHTOWELS HAVE A LOOP OF TWILL TAPE SEWN
INTO THE CORNER TO HANG THEM. THE BUTTONHOLE STITCH CONTINUES IN THE FORM OF "SATIN
STITCH" STRIPES THAT EMBELLISH THE BORDERS. THERE ARE OTHER DECORATIVE OPTIONS YOU
MIGHT WANT TO TRY, TOO. MAKE THE STRIPES DIFFERENT COLORS OR EXPERIMENT WITH DIFFERENT
STRIPE WIDTHS. WHEN GIVING AS A GIFT, I LIKE TO PRESENT THEM AS A SET OF THREE.

MATERIALS

¾ yard (68.6cm) linen/cotton blend or cotton

Note: 60" (152cm) width will make 3 dishtowels

Fabric marker

Sewing thread in 3 different colors, for decorative
embellishment

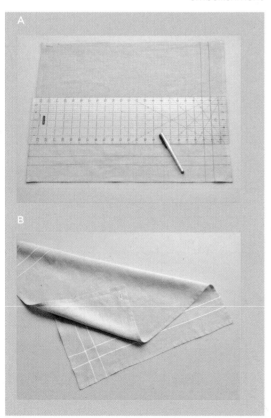

INSTRUCTIONS

Cut 3 rectangles, each 20" × 25" (51 × 63.5cm),
to make 3 dishtowels.

Sew ¼" (6mm) double hems along each edge
of each rectangle.

Mark a vertical buttonhole at the upper-right corner, ½" (13mm) from each edge.

Mark 2 horizontal lines along the bottom edge
of the dishtowel. Mark one line 2" (5cm) from
the edge and one line 3" (7.5cm) from the edge.
These will be decorative stripes.

Mark 2 vertical lines along the left edge of the
dishtowel. Mark one line 2" (5cm) from the edge
and one line 3" (7.5cm) from the edge. These
will also be decorative stripes. **(A)**

Change the sewing thread to a contrasting color.

Set sewing machine to a zigzag stitch and sew
a 1" (2.5cm) vertical buttonhole (instructions on
page 14).

Set the stitch width to the widest measurement
and sew the decorative stripes with a satin
stitch, a wide, tight zigzag. **(B)**

fabric box

THIS BOX CAN HOLD A SMALL GIFT AND ALSO BE A BEAUTIFUL GIFT AFTER IT'S EMPTY! A FABRIC BOX ALONE IS AN INTRIGUING VESSEL: CONSIDER MAKING A SET OF THESE IN DECREASING SIZES, SO THAT THEY FIT ONE INSIDE THE OTHER. IF YOU'RE SEWING JUST ONE, MAKE A LITTLE NEST OF VIBRANTLY COLORED TISSUE PAPER TO SET THE GIFT IN. I FIND IT SO SATISFYING TO SEW SOMETHING THAT TURNS INTO AN AUTOMATIC SCULPTURE, AND JUST THINK OF ALL THOSE COOL PRINTED QUILTING FABRICS OUT THERE JUST WAITING TO BECOME BOXES.

MATERIALS

⅛ yard (11.4cm) printed fabric

Note: You will need about a 5½″ × 35½″ (14 × 90.1cm) strip to make a 4½″ (11.4cm) square box with lid

¼ yard (22.9cm) stiff, fusible interfacing (white for light fabrics; black for dark fabrics)

A

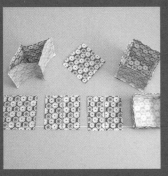

B

INSTRUCTIONS

Lay out the fabric on an ironing surface, wrong-side up. Place the fusible interfacing (5½″ × 35½″ [14 × 90.1cm] strip) over the fabric, shiny (glue) side down. Press with a dry iron and press cloth until the two materials are fused together.

Trim the fused fabric strip so it measures 5″ × 35″ (12.5 × 90cm).

Cut the strip into 8 squares, each measuring 5″ × 5″ (12.5 × 12.5cm). Five squares will make the box and 3 squares will make the lid.

TO MAKE THE BOX

Sew 4 squares in a row, fabric sides together, and sew each with a ¼″ (6mm) seam allowance. End each stitch ¼″ (6mm) from the edge. **(A)**

Sew the first and last square together, making a loop.

Pin a square to the bottom of the box (the side that has seams ¼″ [6mm] from the edge) and sew with a ¼″ (6mm) seam allowance, stopping and starting again at each corner. **(B)**

Trim the corners, turn right-side out, and push out the corners.

Sew a ¼″ (6mm) hem around the top of the box.

TO MAKE THE LID

Cut 2 squares in half to make 4 strips, each measuring 2½″ × 5″ (6.5 × 12.5cm).

Sew the short ends of 4 strips in a row, fabric sides together, and sew each with a ¼″ (6mm) seam allowance. Sew the first and last strip to connect. End the stitch ¼″ (6mm) from the edge.

Pin a square to the top of the lid (the side that has seams $\frac{1}{4}$" (6mm) from the edge), fabric sides facing, and sew with a $\frac{1}{4}$" (6mm) seam allowance, stopping and starting again at each corner.

Trim the corners, turn right-side out, and push out the corners.

Sew a $\frac{1}{4}$" (6mm) hem around the lid. Press edges as close to the corners as you can get. Fill the box with tissue paper to help it keep its shape.

GIF

TS FOR BABIES AND CHILDREN

oilcloth magnets

THESE MAGNETS ARE DESIGNED TO LOOK VERY COOL ON YOUR FRIDGE, ESPECIALLY WHEN LAYERED ON TOP OF EACH OTHER. OILCLOTH IS DURABLE, WATERPROOF, WASHABLE (JUST WIPE WITH A DAMP SPONGE), AND BRIGHTLY COLORED. OILCLOTH IS SLIGHTLY TRANSPARENT, SO TRY TO USE SILVER MAGNETS. IF USING TRADITIONAL DARK-COLORED MAGNETS, GLUE A SMALL PIECE OF OILCLOTH IN BETWEEN THE MAGNET AND THE SHAPE TO CAMOUFLAGE THE DARK SPOT. FOR A GIRLIER LOOK, CHECK OUT THE FLOWER TEMPLATES FROM THE BOTANICAL TIARA PROJECT (PAGE 114). (YOU'LL NEED TO ENLARGE THE TEMPLATES ABOUT 200 PERCENT.) MAGNETS COULD ALSO BE MADE IN OTHER SHAPES, SUCH AS NUMBERS, LETTERS OF THE ALPHABET, OR ANIMALS.

MATERIALS

Three $1/4$ yard (22.9cm) pieces of oilcloth, each in 3 different colors

Button magnets, $1/2$" (13mm) round or smaller

Craft glue (I recommend Gem-Tac glue)

Regular pencil

Template, page 117

INSTRUCTIONS

Transfer the template to a sheet of paper and cut out.

Cut two $5^1/2$" (14cm) squares of oilcloth.

Trace the template with a marker or pencil, marking on the wrong side of one of the oilcloth squares, and cut out.

Apply a drop of glue to a magnet and place it on the wrong side in the center of the cut shape. **(A)**

Place the cut shape over the matching square, wrong sides together, so that the magnet is now inside the two pieces of the oilcloth.

Sew the two pieces together, stitching around the edges of the shape, about $1/8$" (3mm) from the edge.

Cut off the remaining oilcloth, refining the shape if you like. **(B)**

Repeat this process, using different shapes and different colors of oilcloth.

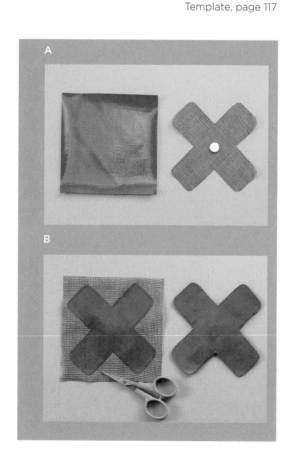

quilted baby blanket

ONE DAY I DECIDED THAT I WANTED TO MAKE "THE AMAZING BABY BLANKET," ONE THAT WAS LUXURIOUS AND BEAUTIFUL BUT SWEET AND COMFY, SOMETHING THAT WOULD BE AN HEIRLOOM BLANKET. I MADE THIS WITH MY FAVORITE FABRICS: HANDKERCHIEF LINEN FOR ONE SIDE AND COTTON FLANNEL FOR THE OTHER. THE QUILTED CIRCLES ARE AN EASY VARIATION ON TRAPUNTO, THE TRADITIONAL QUILTING TECHNIQUE THAT INVOLVES STUFFING SECTIONS OF THE FABRIC. IF YOU WANT TO CHANGE THE DESIGNS, STICK TO SIMPLE ONES, AS TOPSTITCHING SHOULD BE DONE SLOWLY AND CAREFULLY. IT'S VERY IMPORTANT TO USE A FINE-POINT, DISAPPEARING-INK PEN WHEN MARKING THE FABRIC. THIS BLANKET IS SO SOFT, PUFFY, AND CLOUD-LIKE THAT BABIES AND ADULTS ALIKE WILL LOVE IT.

MATERIALS

1 yard (91.4cm) handkerchief or other fine linen

1 yard (91.4cm) cotton flannel

$^1/_4$ yard (22.9cm) batting ($^3/_8$" [9.5mm] thick is ideal)

Fabric marker, fine point, disappearing ink

Hand-sewing needle

Template, see page 118

INSTRUCTIONS

TO PREPARE THE QUILTED DESIGNS

Transfer the templates to paper and cut out.

Pin the templates to the batting and cut out with about an extra $^3/_8$" (9.5mm) added to the edges of the patterns. This is to ensure that the batting gets stitched down and held in place. **(A)**

Cut one 36" × 36" (91.4 × 91.4cm) piece of linen and one 36" × 36" (91.4 × 91.4cm) piece of flannel.

Arrange the templates (or your own designs) on the linen piece, keeping in mind that there is a $^1/_2$" (13mm) seam allowance on all 4 sides of the linen. The circle templates in this blanket are about $2^1/_2$" (6.5cm) from the edge and $2^1/_4$" (5.5cm) apart from each other.

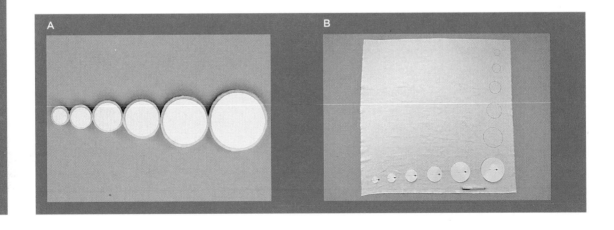

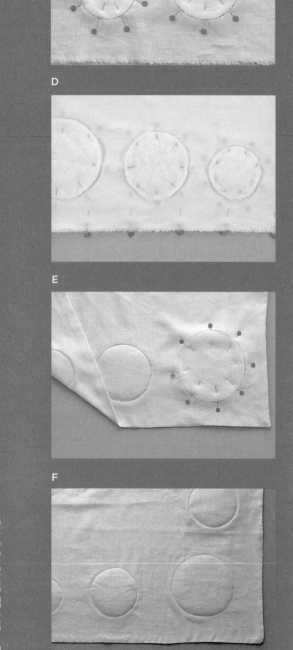

quilted baby blanket

Secure templates to the fabric by pinning them in the center. Trace the designs with a fabric marker and remove the templates. **(B)**

Pin the batting pieces onto the underside of the linen, centering them beneath each corresponding drawn circle. (Another option is to baste the batting into place instead.)

You should be able to see the batting through the linen, or at least feel it. Pin with pinpoints facing in, perpendicular to the stitch line. Use as many pins as you need to secure the batting well.

The side with the line drawings and pins is the right side of the fabric. This is the side to be top-stitched. There should be an extra $^3/_8$" (9.5mm) of the batting beyond the edges of the line drawing to ensure that the filling gets stitched down and held in place. **(C)**

TO MAKE THE BLANKET
Pin the linen and flannel pieces with the right sides facing together. The pins attaching the batting should be on the inside, the batting itself should be on the outside. **(D)**

Sew all sides with a $^1/_2$" (13mm) seam allowance, leaving an 8" (20.5cm) opening at one end.

Trim corners (and excess fabric from seam allowance if needed) and very carefully (watch out for the pins!) turn right-side out. Push out the corners. **(E)**

Press all the edges and the center of the blanket with a hot steam iron, using a press cloth.

Topstitch each design very slowly and carefully, making sure to catch the edges of the batting sandwiched inside. **(F)**

Hand-sew the opening closed and press the entire blanket to finish.

gingham bear bib

CROSS-STITCHING ON GINGHAM WAS A POPULAR DECORATIVE SEWING TECHNIQUE, ESPECIALLY FOR APRONS, IN THE '40S AND '50S. MANY APRONS WERE EMBELLISHED WITH COMBINATIONS OF CROSS-STITCH IN VARIOUS COLORS AND STYLES. THE FACT THAT YOU'RE WORKING ON AN ACTUAL GRID HERE MAKES CROSS-STITCH A PERFECT MATCH FOR GINGHAM. THE BEAUTY OF IT, TOO, IS THAT SIMPLE STITCHES CAN RESULT IN BEAUTIFUL, ELABORATE-LOOKING DESIGNS. THE LOOK OF THE CROSS-STITCH CAN CHANGE DEPENDING ON WHERE YOU POSITION IT ON THE GINGHAM AND WHAT COLOR THREAD YOU CHOOSE. THE BIB TEMPLATE HERE IS ADAPTABLE; THE TEDDY BEAR FACE CAN EASILY BE TURNED INTO MANY OTHER ANIMALS—CAT, PANDA, OR PIG—WITH JUST A FEW MINOR CHANGES. TRY YOUR OWN DESIGNS, USE AN INITIAL, OR SPELL OUT A NAME.

MATERIALS

½ yard (45.7cm) gingham:
8" × 10" (20.5 × 25.5cm) for newborn bib and
8" × 14" (20.5 × 35.5cm) for toddler bib

½ yard (45.7cm) terrycloth:
8" × 10" (20.5 × 25.5cm) for newborn bib and
8" × 14" (20.5 × 35.5cm) for toddler bib

Hook-and-loop tape (Velcro), ½" (13mm) dots

6" (15cm) embroidery hoop, or smaller (optional)

Embroidery floss, 2 or more colors

Fabric marker

Hand-sewing needles, 1 regular and 1 with a large eye, for embroidery floss

Template (represents a quadrant of the bib), page 119

Cross-stitch guide (for bear face), page 120

Hand-sewing needle

INSTRUCTIONS

Enlarge the half-bib pattern and transfer it to a sheet of paper. Cut out to use as the template. Create a full-bib pattern by tracing the template onto a folded piece of paper, adding any extra length you desire. Round off the bottom corners slightly and unfold to see full pattern. Round off more by cutting until you are happy with its shape.

Trace the pattern onto the terrycloth and cut out just the border, leaving the neck hole intact.

Center pattern on a stripe on a piece of gingham, trace and cut out. I find it easier to cut the neck straps (at the center, into halves) after the embroidery is finished.

TO EMBROIDER A DESIGN

To determine the placement of the bear face on the gingham bib, cut an extra piece of gingham, 13 squares high and 17 squares across—the size of the bear face. Move it around, center it, whatever you like. Mark it with the bear-face chart if it's helpful. (Use a regular pen!) Once you've positioned the design, mark the gingham bib with the bear face using a fabric pen. (A)

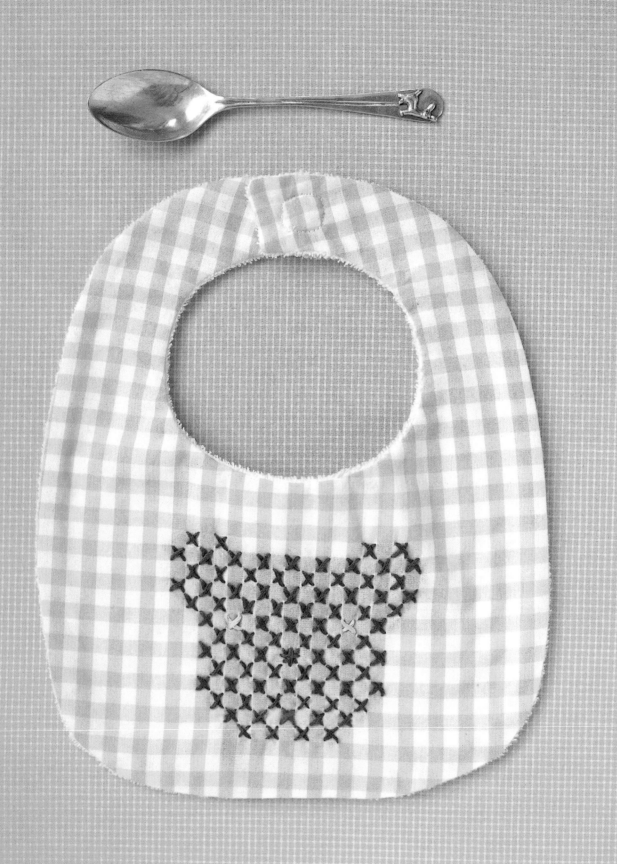

gingham bear bib

Stretch the gingham in an embroidery hoop.

Starting at one corner of the design, sew diagonal stitches on every marked square in that row.

When you reach the last square, turn around and sew diagonal stitches in the opposite direction, making an *X*. **(B)**

When you get to the nose, sew 4 straight stitches to make a star.

Continue sewing row by row, making sure to skip the squares for the eyes and mouth. **(C)**

Once you've completed all the stitches, switch colors to sew the eyes and mouth.

TO MAKE THE BIB
Cut the neck strap of the gingham piece in half, at the center, before pinning to the terrycloth.

Pin the gingham to the terrycloth, right sides facing, and begin sewing at the bottom of the bib, with a 1/4" (6mm) seam allowance. Sew slowly around the curves, leaving a 2" (5cm) opening at the bottom. **(D)**

Cut the remaining terrycloth fabric at the neck hole.

Cut a few slashes into the seam allowance at the curved areas. Turn right-side out and push out the edges.

Press and hand-sew the opening closed.

Sew hook-and-loop tape onto either side of the bib straps.

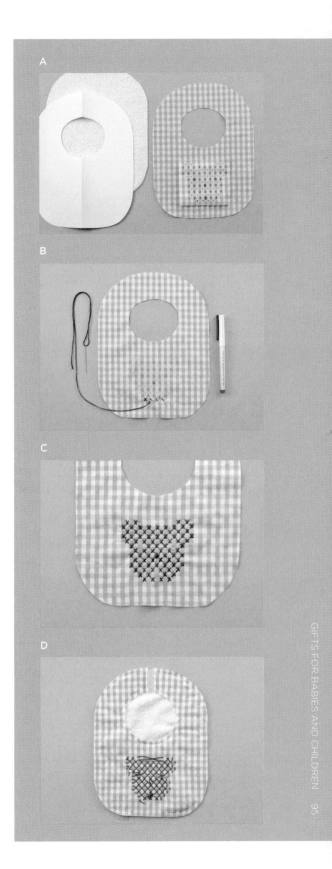

baby bubble hat

HERE IS AN EXAMPLE OF A SIMPLE, CUTE, AND PRACTICAL BABY GIFT. PICK THE SOFTEST COTTON JERSEY, COTTON/RAYON BLEND, OR COTTON/SILK BLEND YOU CAN FIND, AND BY ALL MEANS, STAY AWAY FROM SYNTHETICS! AND BY THE WAY, RAYON IS NOT A SYNTHETIC FIBER: IT IS MADE BY HUMANS, BUT THE MATERIAL ITSELF COMES FROM TREES. BECAUSE THIS HAT IS DESIGNED TO FIT BABIES AGED NEWBORN TO THREE MONTHS OLD, IT MAKES A GREAT BABY SHOWER GIFT.

MATERIALS

½ yard (45.7cm) thin, soft cotton jersey
Batting or fiber filling
Ballpoint needle for sewing machine (#9 or #11)
Hand-sewing needle
Thimble

INSTRUCTIONS

Cut a 7" × 18" (18 × 45.5cm) rectangle of cotton. The cotton should stretch horizontally along the 7" (18cm) side.

Press a ¼" (6mm) hem at the 2 short edges, then press a 1½" (3.8cm) hem. It's easier if you press the hem before sewing the side seams and then fold it up. This hem will end up on the inside of the hat.

With right sides together and the pressed hem laying open, fold the cotton in half crosswise so it measures 7" × 9" (18 × 23cm).

Pin and sew both sides with a ¼" (6mm) seam allowance. Make sure to use a ballpoint needle in the sewing machine. (A)

Fold up the pressed hem and pin the hem, spacing the pins about 1" (2.5cm) apart.

Sew the hem as close as possible to the interior folded hem edge, about ⅛" (3mm) or less. Pull the fabric slightly while sewing, to ensure enough stretch for the hat. Clip the corners and turn the hat right-side out.

Place 2 small balls of batting in each corner.

Cinch the fabric at the base of each ball. Push the needle through the cinched fabric and sew 5 or 6 stitches until the ball is secure. (B)

Lastly, fold up the bottom edge to create a banded brim and press.

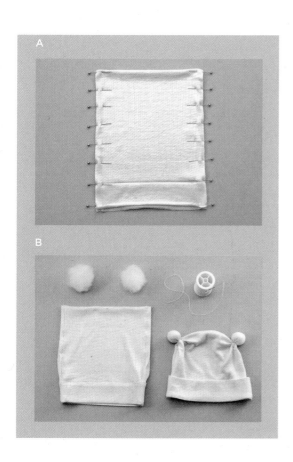

fleece imp hat
& mittens

POLAR FLEECE IS A WONDERFUL MODERN FABRIC THAT IS ESPECIALLY EASY TO WORK WITH BECAUSE, LIKE FELT, IT DOESN'T FRAY. IT'S AVAILABLE IN LOTS OF KID-FRIENDLY COLORS AND WILL KEEP TOTS TOASTY AND WARM ALL WINTER LONG. IT IS IMPORTANT TO DISTINGUISH THE RIGHT SIDE FROM THE WRONG SIDE OF FLEECE WHEN SEWING WITH IT. THE WRONG SIDE HAS A BIT MORE OF A FELTED LOOK TO IT THAN THE RIGHT SIDE DOES. ALWAYS MARK YOUR PATTERN PIECES ON THE WRONG SIDES SO YOU KNOW WHICH SIDE IS WHICH. BECAUSE POLAR FLEECE HAS SOME STRETCH, THESE PATTERNS WILL FIT A ONE- TO THREE-YEAR-OLD CHILD.

MATERIALS

½ yard (45.7cm) polar fleece

Thick yarn

Hand-sewing needle with a very large eye, for yarn

Thimble

10" (25.5) length of elastic, ¼" (6mm) width

Tailor's chalk

Quilting pins (helpful, but not necessary)

Template for hat, page 121

Template for mittens, page 122

INSTRUCTIONS

TO MAKE THE HAT

Enlarge the hat template 145 percent. Cut out to use as the pattern.

Fold the polar fleece in half. Pin paper hat template to polar fleece and cut out through both layers to cut two pieces.

Mark the wrong sides of both pieces with tailor's chalk.

Pin two pieces together, wrong sides facing, and hand-sew together with large whipstitches, each about 1" (2.5cm) apart around the edges. Start the first stitch with the knot 1" (2.5cm) from the edge. Go backwards then forwards to continue stitching (this way the knot is hidden). (A)

When ready to knot the end, sew 1 or 2 stitches back to hide the knot.

Cut ¼" (6mm) holes on both sides of the hat for the chin ties, and pull a 36"- (91.4cm-) long piece of yarn through each hole.

Pull the 2 strands taut and twist them both in the same direction, causing the yarns to twist around one another, joining the 2 together. (B)

At the end, tie a small knot to hold the twist. Repeat for second chin tie.

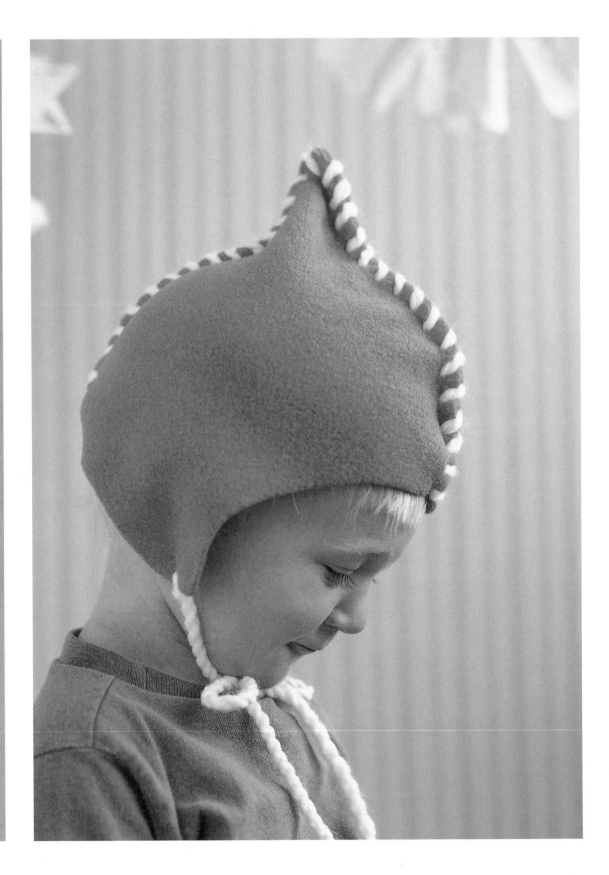

fleece imp hat and mittens

TO MAKE THE MITTENS

Pin the mitten template to a piece of folded polar fleece and cut out through both layers to cut two mittens. Repeat to make a pair.

Match up the pairs and mark the mittens on the wrong side.

Turn and sew a $1/2$″ (13mm) hem on each mitten hand opening. **(C)**

Cut 4 pieces of $1/4$″ (6mm) elastic, each measuring $2^1/2$″ (6.5cm) long.

Set the machine to a zigzag stitch and sew the elastic to the wrong side 1″ (2.5cm) from the hand opening of each mitten. Pull the elastic slightly as you sew so that the elastic gathers the fabric.

Repeat for the other mitten side. Trim off excess elastic. **(D)**

With right sides together, pin edges and sew with a $1/4$″ (6mm) seam allowance. Repeat for the second mitten.

Trim any bulky fabric edges and turn right-side out.

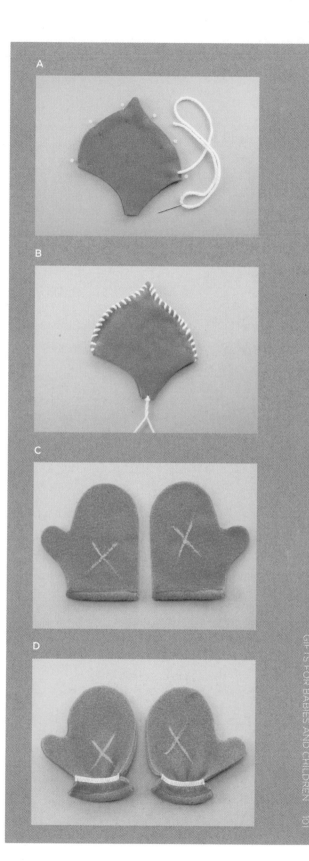

terrycloth bunny

THIS PROJECT COULD BE DONE WITH MANY SOFT FABRICS, BUT BABY STRETCH TERRYCLOTH IS PERFECT HERE BECAUSE OF ITS SOFT, DELICATE TEXTURE AND PASTEL COLOR RANGE. BABY TERRYCLOTH DIFFERS FROM STANDARD TOWEL TERRY; IT'S A THIN, STRETCHY KNIT AND THE FINER LOOPED PILE IS ON ONE SIDE ONLY. WHEN SEWING ON THE EYES, HIDE THE FIRST KNOT UNDER THE STITCHES. FOR A MORE FEMININE BUNNY, LEAVE THE ENDS OF THE KNOT STICKING OUT TO RESEMBLE EYELASHES. ADAPT THE EARS ON THE PATTERN TO MAKE ANY NUMBER OF ANIMALS, SUCH AS A BEAR, CAT, OR MOOSE.

MATERIALS

¼ yard (22.9cm) baby stretch terrycloth

Fabric marker

Polyester fiber filling

Embroidery floss

Hand-sewing needles (1 regular and 1 with a large eye) for embroidery floss

Template, page 123

INSTRUCTIONS

Cut two 4" × 7" (10 × 18cm) pieces of terrycloth and place right sides together.

Pin the template to the wrong side of the fabric. This template does not include a seam allowance, so make sure there is at least ½" (13mm) of fabric around the outside of the template.

Trace the template with a fabric marker. This is the stitching line. Remove the template and pin the fabrics right sides together.

Starting at the bottom of the bunny, sew along the drawn lines. Sew slowly around the curves. Leave a 1" (2.5cm) opening at the bottom.

Cut away any excess material, leaving about a ¼" (6mm) seam allowance and leaving a ½" (13mm) seam allowance at the opening. **(A)**

Turn bunny right-side out. Gently push out the shape and fill with fiber filling. Hand-sew the opening closed.

Draw 2 eyes with a fabric marker. Sew several straight stitches of embroidery floss to make the eyes. **(B)**

magic rain poncho

PONCHOS ARE GREAT BECAUSE ONE DESIGN CAN FIT A VARIETY OF SIZES. IT'S ESSENTIALLY A RECTANGLE WITH A HOLE CUT INTO THE CENTER TO FIT OVER THE HEAD. THIS ONE IS DESIGNED TO FIT CHILDREN AGED ONE TO THREE YEARS. WHEN DESIGNING A PONCHO FOR A LARGER CHILD, ADD TO THE LENGTH (HERE IT MEASURES 20" [51CM] FROM THE SHOULDER TO THE BOTTOM) AND TRIM LESS MATERIAL FROM THE SIDES (HERE I TRIM 2½" [6.5CM] OFF EACH SIDE). WHEN IRONING THE VINYL, BE VERY AWARE OF THE IRON'S CONTACT WITH THE FABRIC. IT SHOULD NOT TOUCH IT AT ALL OR IT WILL MELT INSTANTLY. IT'S A GOOD IDEA TO EXPERIMENT WITH A SMALL PIECE AS A TEST. THE "MAGIC" OF THIS PROJECT IS THE INSTANT TEXTILE YOU CAN CREATE WITH MATERIALS SANDWICHED UNDER THE VINYL. OTHER MATERIALS YOU MIGHT USE INCLUDE FABRIC SCRAPS, EMBROIDERY FLOSS, FLAT SEQUINS, OR ANYTHING FLAT AND COLORFUL. THINK OF IT AS A PAINTING.

MATERIALS

1½ yards (1.4m) muslin or any lightweight cotton, 45" (1.1m) wide

Note: You may need more, depending on whether you adjust the size

3 yards (2.7m) matte-finish, iron-on vinyl, 17" (43cm) wide

Tissue-paper confetti or other flat material to place under vinyl

Fabric marker

Small scissors

INSTRUCTIONS

TO MAKE THE MAGIC VINYL

Cut two 15" × 40" (38.1 × 101.6cm) pieces of iron-on vinyl (for the poncho) and one 11" × 22" (28 × 56cm) piece of vinyl (for the hood).

Lay out the muslin and determine how you are going to fit the 3 vinyl pieces on the fabric before continuing.

Remove the paper backing carefully (you will need it later) and place the vinyl on a flat, clean work surface, sticky side up.

Toss or strategically place some paper confetti (or other material) onto the sticky side of the vinyl. **(A)**

Press the confetti with your fingertip to ensure that it is stuck on.

Lay the sticky side of the vinyl over the muslin carefully, starting at one end and gradually adhering it to the fabric. Smooth it out with your hand as you go. The 3 pieces should fit on 1½ yards (1.4m) of fabric.

Repeat with the other 2 pieces, leaving about 1" (2.5cm) in between each vinyl piece.

Cut out the vinyl/cotton pieces, cutting in between, where there is no vinyl (no need to be precise since they will be trimmed later).

Press the vinyl side of the pieces. Lay the paper backing (peeled off earlier), shiny side down, over the vinyl and press with a dry iron set on a medium temperature. This will ensure adhesion of the vinyl.

Turn over and press the cotton side of the fabric, without the paper. The vinyl should be adhered well now. If not, press until it is.

Trim the vinyl pieces, cutting away any muslin that is not coated with vinyl.

TO MAKE THE PONCHO

Pin the 2 large pieces along the long edges, vinyl sides together, spacing the pins about 8″ (20.5cm) apart, and sew with a $1/2$″ (13mm) seam allowance.

Press the cotton side, with the seam folded to one side, using the paper to protect the vinyl on the seam. Press the seam on the vinyl side, using the paper as before. You should have a large vinyl/cotton rectangle, measuring 28″ x 40″ (71 x 101.6cm). **(B)**

Position the seam at the center front and back of poncho.

Sew a $1/4$″ (6mm) double hem on all 4 sides. This will be the poncho.

Mark the center point of the poncho by folding in quarters.

Mark 4″ (10cm) from the center point, vertically and horizontally. Connect the marked points to form a diamond. Cut out carefully, using a small scissors. This is the neck opening. **(C)**

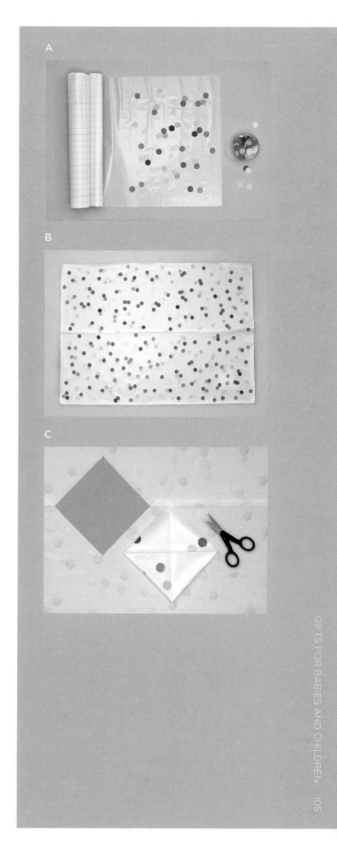

Sew double $\frac{1}{4}$" (6mm) hems on one long side of the 11" × 22" (28 × 56cm) piece. Fold crosswise, vinyl sides together. Sew the edge opposite the hemmed edge to create the hood. Sew with a $\frac{1}{4}$" (6mm) seam allowance. **(D)**

With right sides together, pin the hood to the poncho neck opening, aligning the seams and easing to fit. Pin around the 3" (7.6cm) corners carefully. **(E)**

Sew with a $\frac{1}{4}$" (6mm) seam allowance.

Sew the remaining raw edge at the front of the opening with a $\frac{1}{4}$" (6mm) seam allowance. **(F)**

Turn the poncho and hood right-side out.

leaf cushion

HERE, THE LEAF IS REDUCED TO ITS SIMPLEST ICONIC SHAPE, ENHANCED BY THE CORDUROY TO GIVE THE IMPRESSION OF THE LEAF'S VEINS. THIS FABRIC IS AVAILABLE IN MANY WALES (WIDTH OF RIDGES); I USE A WIDE-WALE CORDUROY HERE. IT MAKES THE LEAF VEINS MORE GRAPHIC. CORDUROY IS SOFT AND DURABLE, AND IT COMES IN SO MANY COLORS. BECAUSE THESE CUSHIONS ARE MEANT TO BE SAT UPON, STUFF THE LEAVES AS FULL AS YOU CAN BECAUSE THE FIBER FILLING WILL SETTLE OVER TIME. MAKE MANY, IN VARIOUS SIZES AND COLORS, TO SCATTER ALL OVER THE FLOOR.

MATERIALS

1 yard (91.4cm) corduroy, 58" (1.5m) wide

Note: 1 yard will make 3 cushions

Polyester fiber filling

Hand-sewing needle

Large sheet of paper, 18" × 24" (45.5 × 61cm), to accommodate the full leaf pattern

Template ($^1/_4$ of the leaf), page 124

INSTRUCTIONS

Enlarge template 135 percent, and trace onto a large sheet of paper, folded in quarters. Cut out and unfold for full leaf pattern. You may also choose to use the template as a visual reference and cut freehand.

Fold the corduroy in half, wrong sides together, and lay the pattern at a 45-degree angle. Pin the pattern to the folded fabric and cut out. (A)

Cut both leaves in half, vertically. Switch the leaf halves, pairing them so when put together, the corduroy lines mirror each other. (B)

Pin leaf halves together, along the vertical line only, right sides facing together, and sew $^1/_4$" (6mm) seam allowance. Press the seams open with a hot iron.

Pin the leaves, right sides together, and sew all the edges with a 2" (13mm) seam allowance, leaving a 5" (12.5cm) opening.

Trim the seam edges at the tips, turn right-side out, and push out the tips.

Press the fabric at the opening (mimicking the seam allowance). Stuff with fiber filling and hand-sew the opening closed.

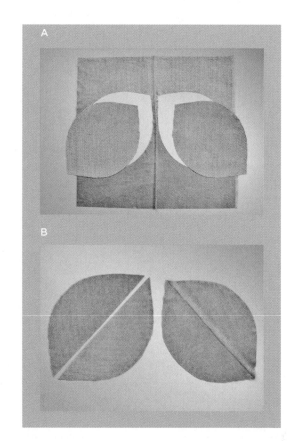

sewn star card

THIS CARD ACCOMPANIED THE BIRTH ANNOUNCEMENT SENT OUT WHEN MY SON WAS BORN. IT WAS INSPIRED BY HAND-LACED SEWN CARDS. I LIKE USING TRANSPARENT VELLUM FOR THIS PROJECT; THE CARD LOOKS BEAUTIFUL AND LUMINOUS WHEN LIGHT SHINES THROUGH IT.

MATERIALS

Medium-weight transparent vellum or cardstock

Note: An 8½" × 11" (21.5 × 28cm) sheet will make 2 cards

Lightweight paper, white or light color

Note: An 8½" × 11" (21.5 × 28cm) sheet will make 2 card linings

Easy-to-remove tape such as drafting tape

Mat knife or rotary cutter

Template, page 125

Note: This card will fit a standard size A2 envelope

INSTRUCTIONS

Cut card paper in half crosswise to measure 5½" × 8½" (14 × 21.5cm).

Cut one 5¼" × 8¼" (13.3 × 21cm) piece of lining paper.

Score the card paper and lining paper at the halfway crosswise point and fold in half.

Lightly tape the lining paper to the card paper, positioning it in the center. Tape the star template to the front of the card by placing the tape under the center of star. **(A)**

Set the sewing machine to a "down needle" position. This will make it easy to pivot at the angles.

Starting at the top of the star's point, begin to stitch around the template. Do not back-tack.

When you are finished, do not back-tack, and leave a tail of about 5" (12.5cm) of thread at the start and end point.

Tie the threads together on both the inside and outside trup of the card to lock in the stitches. **(B)**

A

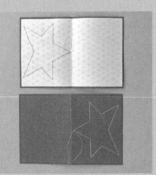

B

Templates and Guides

The following templates and guides accompany projects from all the chapters. To create a pattern from a template, simply trace the template onto a piece of paper and, where indicated, enlarge using a photocopier.

ROUND LEAF

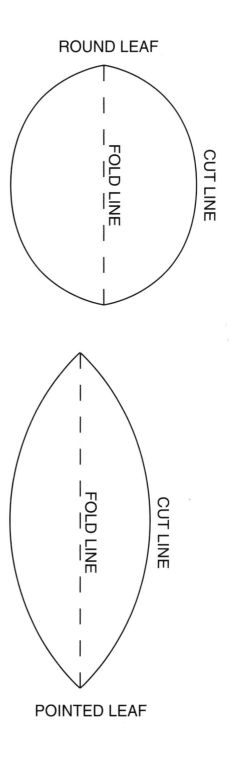

FOLD LINE

CUT LINE

ROUND FLOWER

CUT LINE

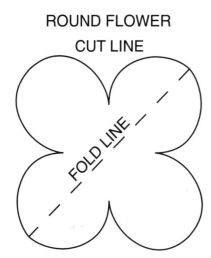

FOLD LINE

POINTED FLOWER

CUT LINE

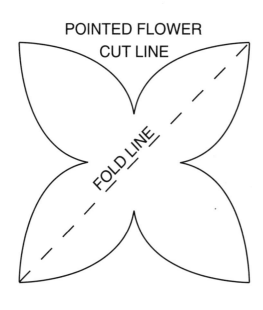

FOLD LINE

FOLD LINE

CUT LINE

POINTED LEAF

CUT LINE

OVERLAP LINE

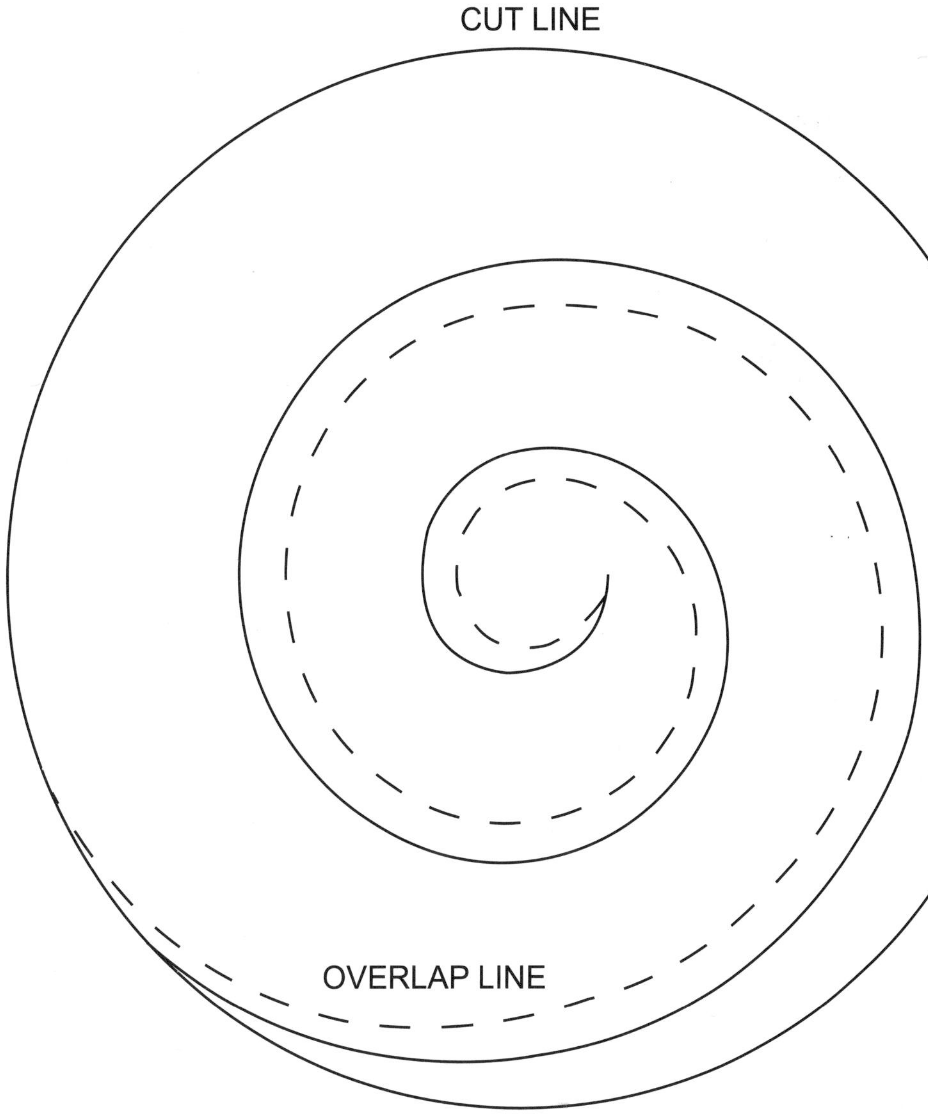

Page 77
Use as measurement guide only

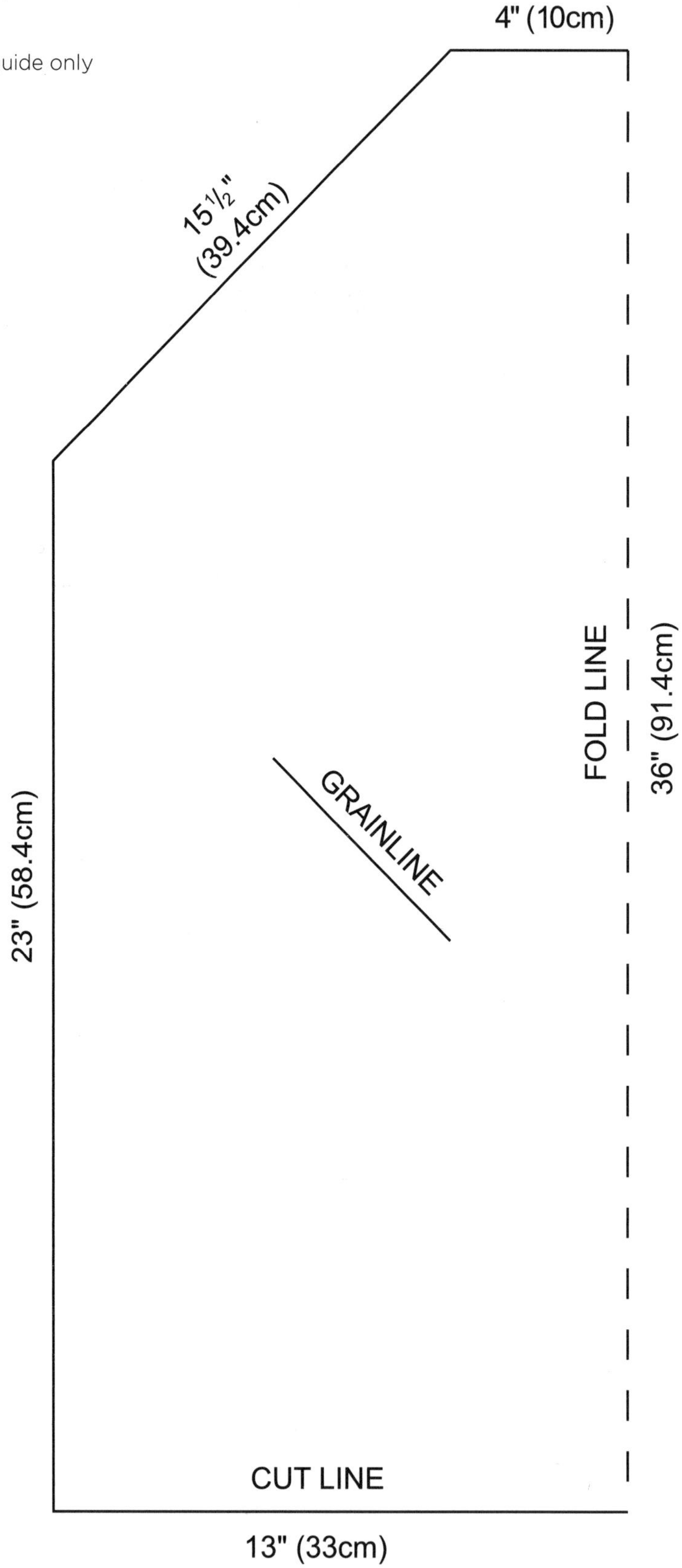
4" (10cm)
15½"
(39.4cm)
FOLD LINE
36" (91.4cm)
GRAINLINE
23" (58.4cm)
CUT LINE
13" (33cm)

CUT LINE

STITCH LINES

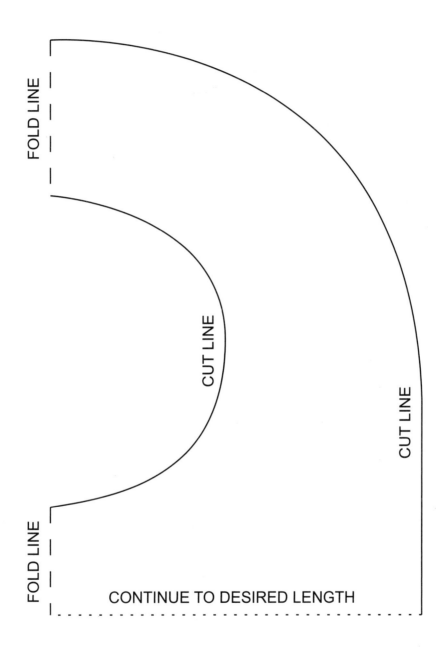

FOLD LINE

FOLD LINE

CUT LINE

CUT LINE

CONTINUE TO DESIRED LENGTH

1 SQUARE = 1 STITCH

17 STITCHES

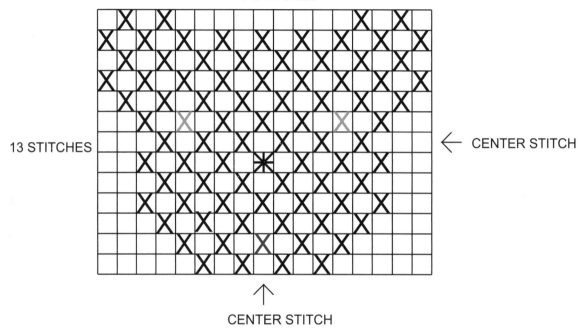

13 STITCHES

← CENTER STITCH

↑
CENTER STITCH

☒ CROSS-STITCH WITH BODY COLOR

☒ CROSS-STITCH WITH EYE COLOR

☒ CROSS-STITCH WITH MOUTH COLOR

✳ LEVIATHAN STITCH WITH BODY COLOR

CUT LINE

CUT LINE

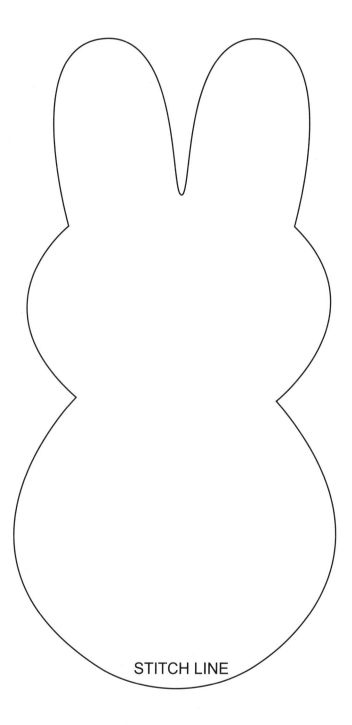

STITCH LINE

LEAF CUSHION

Page 108
Enlarge 145%

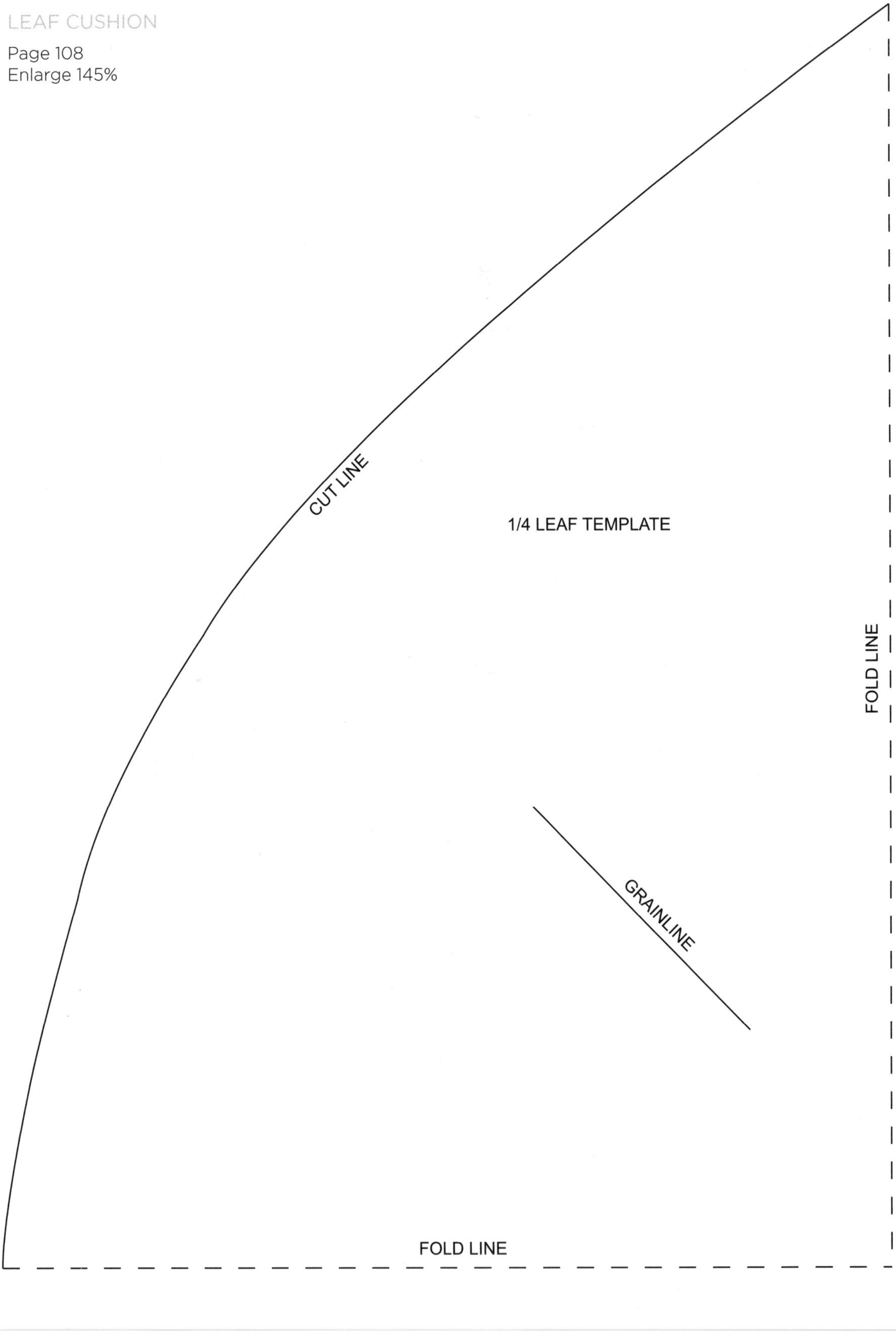
CUT LINE
1/4 LEAF TEMPLATE
FOLD LINE
GRAINLINE
FOLD LINE

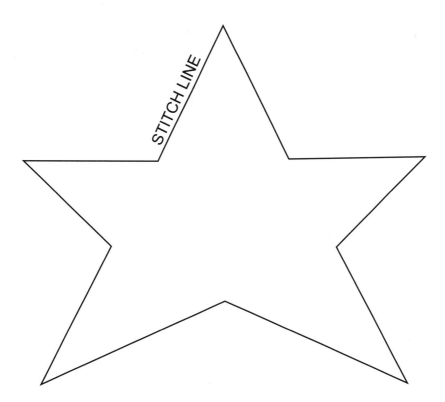

STITCH LINE

acknowledgments

I have many people to thank for help, inspiration, instruction, support, and encouragement on this big project, this book.

My darling rock husband, Jon Hokanson, and our sparkly son, Silas!

My family: My parents, Carolyn and Jim, who gave me a wonderful childhood full of creativity and an art-school education. My sister, Kristin, Jon's sister, Katya, and Jon's parents, Kay and Bill, who all helped brainstorm about cool things to sew.

My friend Hillary Moore, who is really like my sister, I thank you for your brilliant advice and creative ideas, always right on.

Sewing Circle friends Helen Quinn, Jessica Vitkus, Yuh Okano, and Toto Feldman, who all made it a party. Ainslie Street Collective friends Theo Coulombe and Akiko Nishimura, who made it a party, too. Friends and colleagues at *Martha Stewart Living,* who have taught and inspired me over the years. Writers Daniel Petix and

Marek Waldorf and designer Mine Suda, who helped with final touches.

A big thank you to all the people who worked so hard on the production of this book: Editor Rosy Ngo, Editor Christina Schoen, Book Designer Lauren Monchik, Designer Orit Mardkha-Tenzer, Jr. Designer La Tricia Watford, Technical Editor Peggy Greig, Developmental Editor Kathleen Hackett, Copy Editor Betsy Beier, Design Assistant Amy Sly, Photographer Alexandra Grablewski, Stylist Anna Beckman, and Models Nyree Hansen, Yuh Okano, Paul Breen, Ogbitse Omagbemi, Monte Zizzo, and Silas Hokanson.

I am grateful for the generosity of people who provided materials: Lynne Browne at Coats & Clark, Melanie Nerenberg at Kate's Paperie, Cardie Molina at Oilcloth International, Patty Munro at Toray Ultrasuede, Rosemary Kozdra at Malden Mills, Candace Harrington at Thermoweb, Catherine Hurlbut at Fairfield Poly-Fil, and Suzanne Fanning and Patricia Likwarz at Fiskars.

suggested reading

Davis, Tina. See And Sew: *A Sewing Book for Children.* New York: Stewart, Tabori & Chang, 2006. *Brilliant graphic illustrations show a variety of techniques and beginner sewing projects. Designed for children.*

Dupuy, Céline. *Simple Sewing with a French Twist*. New York: Potter Craft, 2006. *A beautifully styled and photographed collection of vivid sewn creations.*

Kirkwood, Janet. *The Complete Book of Needlecraft.* New York: Exeter Books, 1978. *An excellent and comprehensive encyclopedia of stitchery including sewing, embroidery, knitting, and crochet.*

Wolff, Colette. *The Art of Manipulating Fabric.* Radnor, PA: Krause Publications, 1996. *A stunning and hugely extensive exploration of every sewing technique imaginable—all projects created with muslin and photographed in black and white.*

Vitkus, Jessica. *AlternaCrafts: 20+ High-Style Lo-Budget Projects to Make.* New York: Stewart,Tabori & Chang, 2006. *A treasury of avant-garde and classic sewing crafts with a clever emphasis on recycling.*

Yanagi, Soetsu. *The Unknown Craftsman: A Japanese Insight into Beauty.* New York: Kodansha International, 1972. *A profound and philosophical view of the creative process and the importance of craft and the handmade object.*

resources

All of the projects in the book call for materials that are readily available at fabric and craft stores near you. The following list will help you find any fabric, notions, or other supplies you might need to complete the projects.

FABRIC

B & J Fabrics—fabric
212-354-8150
www.bandjfabrics.com
(Store located in New York City)

Fields Fabrics—Fabric
www.fieldsfabrics.com
(Online retailer with locations in West Michigan)

Malden Mills—polar fleece
978-557-3242
www.maldenmillsstore.com
(Online retailer)

Mood Designer Fabric Inc.—fabric
212-730-5003
www.moodfabrics.com
(Store located in New York City)

P and S Fabrics—fabric, notions, trimmings
212-226-1534
www.psyarns.com
(Online retailer with location in New York City)

Rosen & Chadick Fabrics—fabric
212-869-0142
800-225-3838
www.rosenandchadickfabrics.com
(Two-floor showroom located in New York City)

Toray Ultrasuede America—Ultrasuede
www.ultrasuede.com
(Store locator available)

NOTIONS AND SUPPLIES

Coats & Clark—thread
800-648-1479
www.coatsandclark.com
(Store locator available)

Elegant Stitches—cotton, rickrack
888-639-9383
www.elegantstitches.com
(Online retailer with location in Cary, NC)

Fairfield Processing—batting, pillows, fiber filling
800-243-0989
www.poly-fil.com
(Store locator available)

Fiskars Brands Inc.—rotary cutters, scissors, rulers, cutting mats
866-348-5661
www.fiskarscrafts.com
(Online retailer with store locator)

Hyman Hendler and Sons—ribbon
212-840-8393
www.hymanhendler.com
(Store located in New York City)

Kate's Paperie—paper
800-809-9880
www.katespaperie.com
(Online retailer with store locator)

Lee Jofa—wallpaper
(see page 30)
www.leejofa.com
(Showroom locator available)

Oilcloth International—oilcloth
323-344-3967
www.oilcloth.com
(Store locator available)

Therm O Web—iron-on vinyl (Heat 'n' Bond brand)
847-520-5200
www.thermoweb.com
www.mimicollections.com
(Store locator available)

Tinsel Trading—artificial stamens
212-730-1030
www.tinseltrading.com
(Store located in New York City)

Scalamandre—wallpaper
(see pages 69, 96)
www.scalamandre.com
(Showroom locator available)

index